Coral Reef

Ruth Soffer

PUBLISHER'S NOTE

The brilliant colors of coral reefs—green, purple, orange, red, in a broad range of indescribable shades—may be seen for miles and miles in tropical waters in some parts of the world. These reefs have their basis in living creatures called polyps. Coral polyps (or more simply corals), found only in marine environments, are relatively primitive creatures that attach themselves to the ocean floor in calm, shallow tropical waters. Coral polyps all have a ring of tiny tentacles surrounding a central mouth supported on a stem. Minuscule creatures that swim past are stung and eaten. Some types of corals living in huge colonies secrete a hard substance made of limestone, and this builds up over years to create vast reefs. The varied colors of many coral reefs come from neither the living coral nor their limestone deposits, but from algae—tiny plants that survive inside of the corals, benefiting them and benefiting from them in turn.

The sea, and particularly coral reefs, has a variety of life forms broader than in any region of land. Representatives of these creatures are depicted in the drawings that follow in this book. They are divided among the following *phyla* (plural of *phylum,* the largest subdivision in the animal kingdom).

Porifera. These are the sponges, the most primitive animals after the single-celled protozoa. Sponges are multicellular but the cells are not differentiated into distinct tissues or organs.

Cnidaria (or Coelenterates). Cnidaria are slightly less primitive than the sponges. They may be free-swimming or they may live attached to fixed objects. Cnidaria include jellyfish, sea anemones and corals themselves.

Echinodermata. These creatures of many forms are all protected by hard but often flexible shells or skins. Echinoderms are typically divided into five or more segments, although this is not always obvious. This group includes starfish, sea cucumbers, sea urchins and crinoids (like starfish but with long, thin, wavy arms).

Annelida. These are the segmented worms. Unlike the above phyla, which are found only in the sea, Annelida live everywhere—in fresh water, in saltwater and on land. The earthworm is the most familiar annelid. Many very strange types live in the sea, some anchored to a single spot, others free-swimming.

Arthropoda. There are far more arthropods than any other kind of animal. About ninety percent are insects, and many of the rest are spiders, centipedes, etc., none of which is found in coral reefs. Crustaceans, however, are arthropods that *are* found in coral reefs. These include several species of crabs. Other crustaceans include shrimps and lobsters.

Mollusca. Mollusks are another enormous phylum of animals, found in fresh and salt water and on land. Many have hard shells, but many do not. Snails, octopuses, squid, oysters, mussels and clams are all members of the phylum Moll-

Chordata. This large and very varied group includes all of the vertebrates. Chordates are animals with some form of spinal cord (at least at some stage of their development). There are so many chordates that they are divided into many subphyla and classes.

Of those subphyla of chordates represented in this book, that of the Tunicata is the only one that is unfamiliar to most people. Tunicates are small rounded or tubular animals, some types of which fix themselves to the ocean floor or another creature, and then feed on the tiny animals and plants that drift by. Much more primitive than other members of this phylum, tunicates are classified with the chordates because at least in some life stage a simple spinal cord develops in these strange animals.

The other members of the Chordata need little introduction. They include the true vertebrates, animals with developed skeletons: fishes, amphibians, reptiles, birds and mammals. Although most reptiles and mammals live on land, some have adapted to life in the sea and are found around coral reefs. One reptile and one mammal are represented in the drawings in this book.

Of course there is an abundance of fish amid coral reefs. Many are among the most colorful in the world. Don't be afraid to give them lively, shimmering colors in the drawings that follow!

In each of the drawings, the most prominent coral-reef inhabitants depicted are identified by common name and, in most cases, by Latin name.

The **Moorish Idol** (*Zanclus canescens*) lives around Australia's Great Barrier Reef. This exotic-looking fish (growing to about eight inches) is a prized—but hard-to-keep—aquarium fish.

Related to the Seahorse, the strange-looking **Leafy Sea Dragon** (*Phycodurus eques*) is a species of Pipefish that inhabits reefs in the South Sea of Australia.

Here are three varieties of **Nudibranch** (order Nudibranchia) inhabiting Australia's Great Barrier Reef. These brightly colored shell-less snails are mollusks feeding primarily on sea anemones. The Nudibranch at the left (*Jason mirabilis*) is covered with spines. At the top right is the **Spanish Dancer Nudibranch** (*Hexabranchus sanguineus*).

The **Harlequin Tusk Fish** is a sharp-toothed inhabitant of the Great Barrier Reef.

8

The **Blue Devil** (*Abudefduf cyanea;* top) is a brilliant blue fish, popular as an aquarium fish. The **Sea Tulip, Ascidian, Tunicate** or **Sea Squirt** (right), as it is variously called, is a strange creature (order Ascidiacea of the subphylum Tunicata) that looks like a plant but is an animal, and actually has a primitive backbone in the larval stage. Sea Tulips feed by filtering small creatures from the water. At the bottom are two **Studded Starfish** (phylum Echinodermata). (South Sea, Australia.)

Lionfish (*Pterois volitans*). This strange-looking fish (also from Suruga Bay) is very graceful and dignified in its behavior. Its spines are as fearsome as they look, being highly poisonous. It eats mostly crabs.

Center: **Cherry Blossom Anthius** (*Anthius* sp.). This colorful fish lives in Suruga Bay (Japan). The tentacle-waving **Cerianthid** (phylum Cnidaria) is a nocturnal coral-building creature that looks like and is related to the anemones.

11

The **Blue-ringed Octopus** (*Hapalochlaena maculosa*) is also a mollusk—
a poisonous member of its family dwelling in Australia's South Sea.

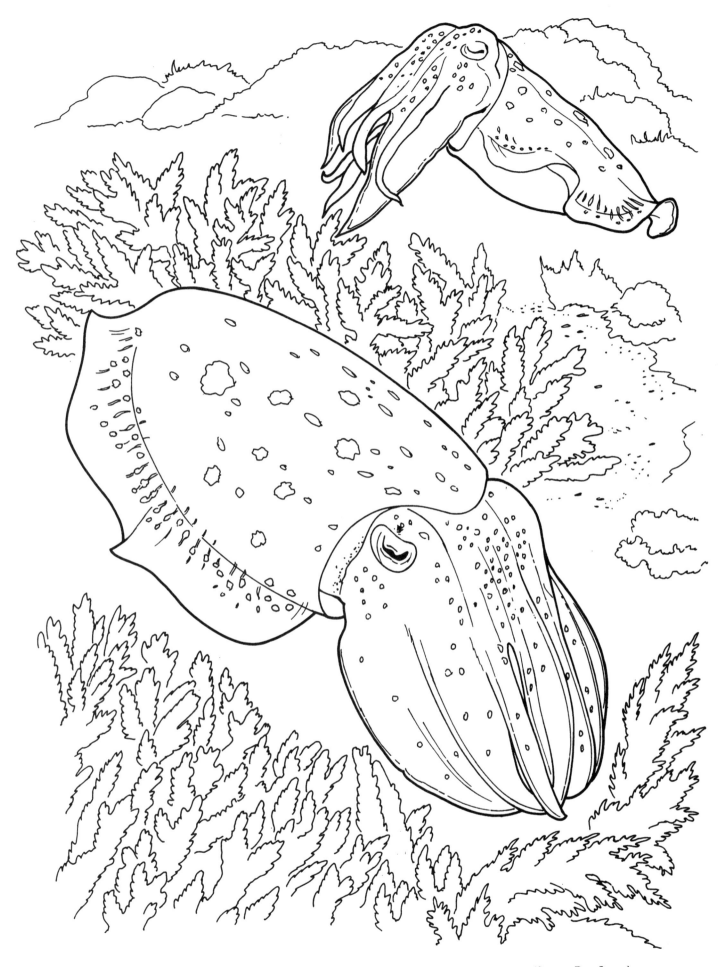

Cuttlefish (order Sepioidea). This mollusk is closely related to squids and octopuses (Suruga Bay, Japan).

Spotted Triggerfish (*Balistoides viridescens*). The spots of this triggerfish are not always clearly visible. The sharp teeth of all triggerfish enable them to crush the shells and hard crusts of the creatures they feed on. (Red Sea.)

Royal Empress Angelfish (*Pygoplites diacanthus*). This is a royal-looking fish indeed, its coloring a striking contrast of blues and yellow. It feeds on sponges and algae, among other small items. (Red Sea.)

Center: **Saddleback Butterflyfish** (*Chaetodon ulietensis*). This black, white and yellow butterflyfish is, like many of its family, popular as an aquarium fish. Upper left: **Snapper** (*Lutjanus* sp.). One of many types of snapper, this fish is common in coral reefs of the Pacific. There are several corals in this drawing. At the left is a **Nephtheid** (family Nephtheidae), a "soft" coral. At the right is **Dendronephthya** (*Dendronephthya* sp.), also a "soft," non-reef-building coral. At the bottom is **Plate Coral** (*Valonia ventricosa*), a "hard" coral. (Great Barrier Reef, Australia.)

On the sea floor is **Star Coral** (*Montastrea cavernosa*). This coral forms mountainous clusters. Above it is a plumelike **Gorgonian** (order Gorgonacea), also a coral, from a group that includes the sea fans and whip corals. The crab at the left is a **Coral Crab** (*Carpilius corallinus*), a very large crustacean with rich red coloring. Finally, there is the **Stone Crab** (*Menippe mercenaria*), a stubby, stonelike red or (when young) purple crab. (Caribbean.)

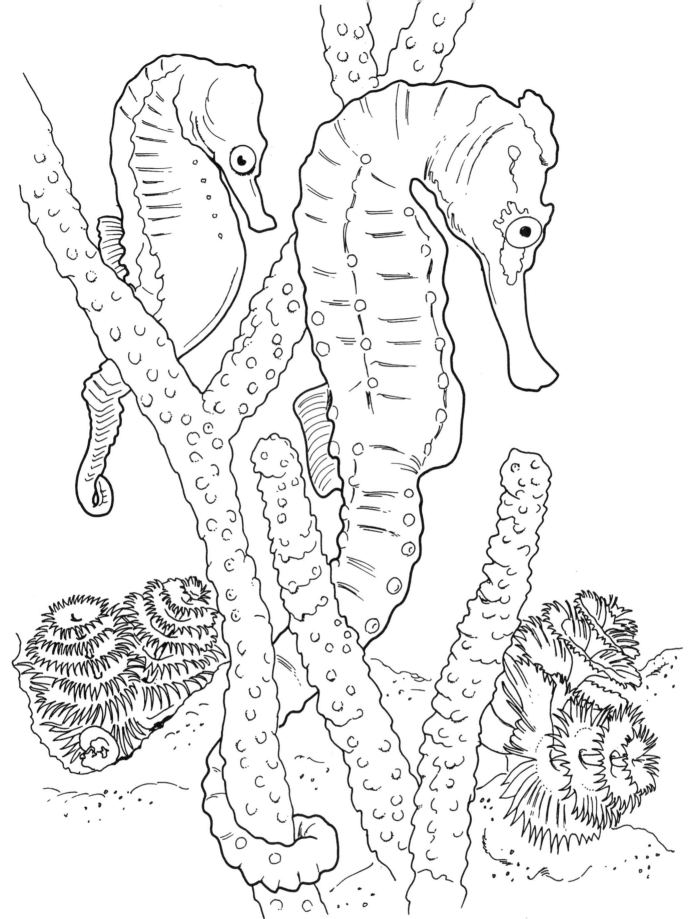

Center: **Seahorse** (*Hippocampus* sp.). This strange small fish is well known from aquariums. It looks like a little horse. It is also unusual in that the male incubates the female's eggs in a pouch. It is wrapped around a **Gorgonian** (order Gorgonacea; see page 17). The **Spiral-gilled Tubeworm** (*Sebellastarte* sp.), bottom, is an annelid. Tubeworms are confined to their tubes, cementlike structures anchored to the ocean floor. They filter food from their surroundings. (Caribbean.)

Bottom: **Elkhorn Coral** (*Acropora palmata*), the most common coral in the Caribbean, forming enormous colonies in shallow waters. Swimming around it is the **Hawksbill Turtle** (*Eretmochelys imbricata*), the only reptile depicted in this book. This shy sea turtle feeds on sponges. (Caribbean.)

Foreground: **Red Clownfish** (*Amphiprion frenatus*). Like all clown—or anemone—fishes, the Red Clownfish lives among the poisonous tentacles of sea anemones. The **Three-spot Damselfish** (*Dascyllus trimaculatus*) is one of many damselfish living among corals and feeding on small crustaceans. The **Sea Anemone** (order Actiniaria) itself is a cnidarian, related to corals. It is familiar for its masses of wavy tentacles. (Red Sea.)

The coral at the bottom is a **Hydro Coral** (*Stylaster roseus*), a hydrozoan, a special class of reef-building corals. Above is a **Scrawled Filefish** (*Cantberbines pullus*), and the large fish in the center is a **Taillight Filefish** (family Melancanthidae). (Caribbean.)

21

This view of a Caribbean coral reef features three kinds of **Butterflyfish** (family Chaetodontidae). The coral shown is a **Sea Fan** (*Gorgonia* sp.), with broad, branching, fanlike structures.

Above: **Stoplight Parrotfish** (*Sparisoma viride*). This fish gets its name from the female's bright red belly and fins. Males, also beautiful, with shades of blue-green and pink and yellow, look very different. Center: **Princess Parrotfish** (*Scarus taeniopterus*), a lovely multicolored fish, orange, yellow and blue in

delicate shades. Behind the fish is **Fire Coral** (order Milleporia). Only distantly related to true corals, fire corals are of a distinct class (Hydrozoa). Brushing against one can cause a painful welt, the tiny polyp colonies injecting poison into the skin. (Caribbean.)

The **Spanish Hogfish** (*Bodianus rufus*). When small, this lovely yellow and brownish red fish eats parasites from the bodies of other fish. Later it switches to tough food such as crabs and sea urchins. Below it are two common starfish called the **Thorny Sea Star** (*Echinaster sentus*). (Caribbean.)

The **Frogfish** (*Antennarius* sp.) is a type of angler fish, and a voracious feeder. Its appearance is bizarre but sometimes strangely beautiful. Bottom: the **Atlantic Purple Sea Urchin** (*Arbacia punctulata*) is an echinoderm, related to starfish. It is a spiny creature that lives on the bottom of the sea. (Caribbean.)

The fish are all **Yellow Damselfish** (*Eupomacentrus planifrons*). This very hardy fish of the Caribbean is yellow with a prominent black spot when young. Above is an adult. Below is

Brain Coral (phylum Cnidaria), one of a group of hard-to-identify stony corals, in a shape like that of a brain. In the background is **Fire Coral** (see page 23).

The mountainous coral at the bottom is a form of **Star Coral** (*Favia fragum*), a yellow or brownish white coral that forms small colonies, each like a loaf of bread. Center: **Porkfish** (*Anisotremus virginicus*). Often found in large schools, this yellow, black and gray fish grows to a foot. (Caribbean.)

Top: **Green Moray Eel** (*Gymnothorox funebris*), a large, brilliantly colored eel with powerful jaws. Below is the **Goldentail Moray Eel** (*Muriaena miliaris*). (Caribbean.)

The fish is of the species **Brown Chromis** (*Chromis multi-lineatus*), a small fish that eats plankton. Bottom, left: **Slate Pencil Urchin** (*Eucidaris tribuloides*), another species of sea urchin. In the background is the **Bushy Gorgonian** (*Plexaura flexuosa*), another coral of the odd group of Gorgonians. (Caribbean.)

Top: **Nassau Grouper** (*Epinephelus striatus*). This fish—unusual even for a Grouper—passes through up to eight color phases with all sorts of different patterns, sometimes all in a few minutes! Below is a **Yellowmouth Grouper** (*Mycteroperca interstitialis*), a little-known, handsome grouper. Growing on the ocean floor is a **Callyspongia Sponge** (*Callyspongia sp.*) (Caribbean.)

Swimming among a number of sponges here is the **Graysby** (*Petrometepon cruentum*), a red-spotted type of Grouper. (Caribbean.)

31

Bluehead (*Thalassoma bifasciatus*). The striking blue head of this yellow wrasse is exhibited only by adult males, shown here. (Caribbean.)

The well-known **Barracuda** (*Sphyraena* sp.). Barracuda may actually be any of several species of fierce predatory fish, growing up to six feet long. They often travel in large schools. (Caribbean.)

Spiny Puffer (*Tetraodon* sp.). Like all puffers this spiny fish puffs itself up to make life difficult for would-be predators. Bottom: before puffing; top: after puffing. (Caribbean.)

Top: the **Barred Hamlet** (*Hypoplectrus puella*). This small but voracious brown-and-white fish is related to the Groupers. It is the most common Hamlet. A much rarer member of the family (below) is the **Shy Hamlet** (*Hypoplectrus guttavarius*), a small, brilliantly colored (orange and black) fish. (Caribbean.)

All three of these fish are **Squirrelfish** (*Holocentrus ascensionis*). These large-eyed fish hide under crevices in coral and rocks and come out at night to feed. (Caribbean.)

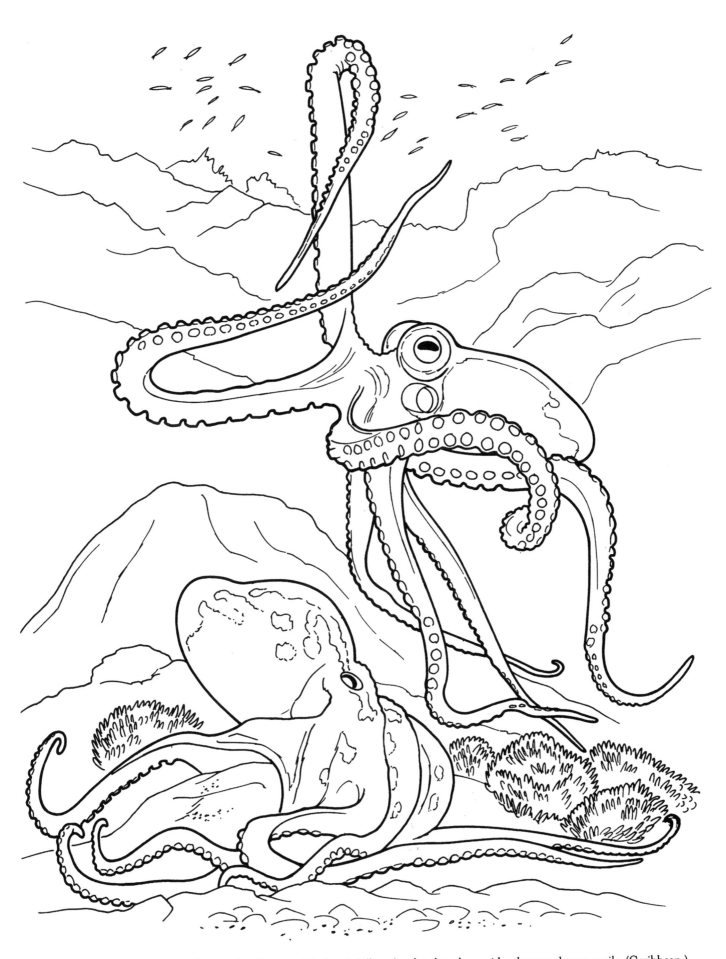

Here is a creature everyone knows: the **Octopus** (phylum Mollusca), related to the squids, clams and even snails. (Caribbean.)

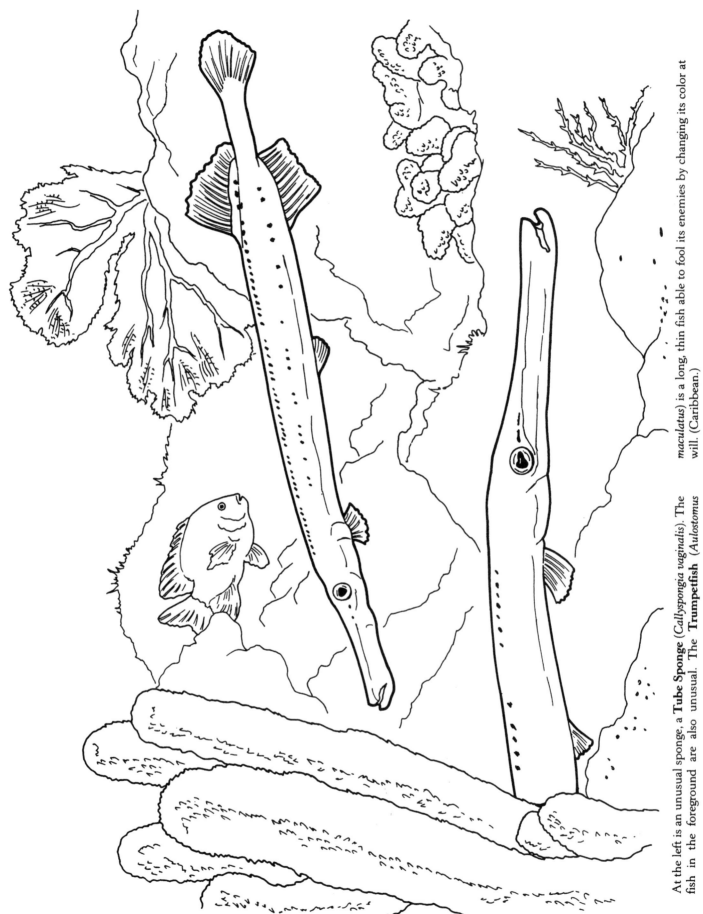

At the left is an unusual sponge, a **Tube Sponge** (*Callyspongia vaginalis*). The fish in the foreground are also unusual. The **Trumpetfish** (*Aulostomus maculatus*) is a long, thin fish able to fool its enemies by changing its color at will. (Caribbean.)

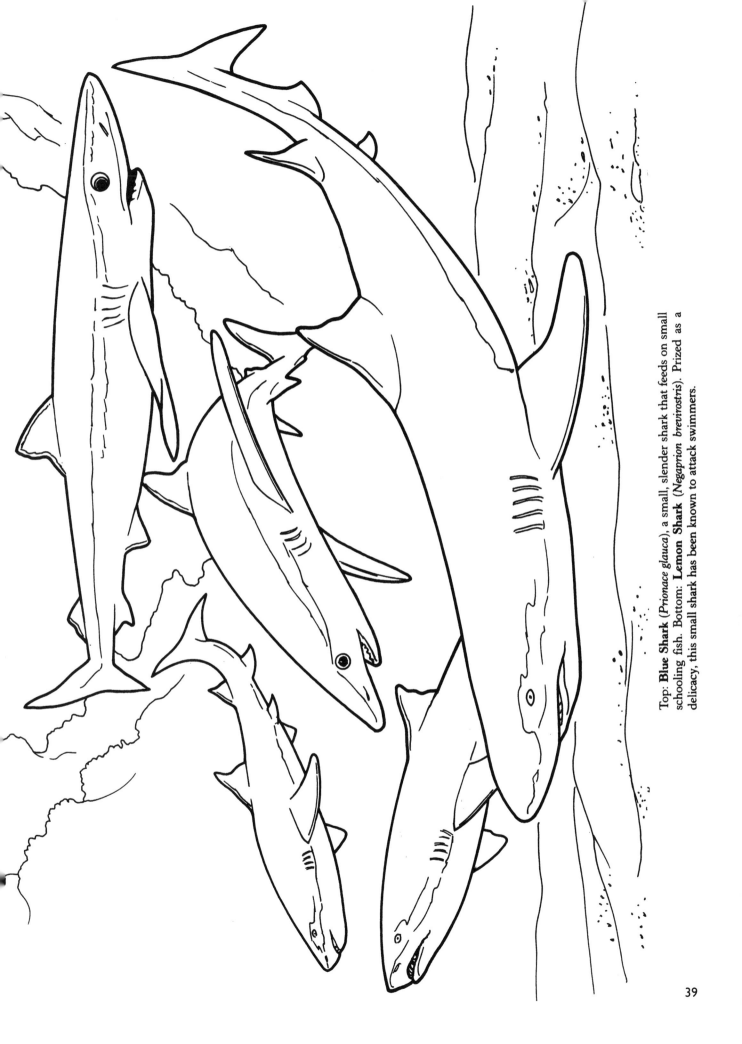

Top: **Blue Shark** (*Prionace glauca*), a small, slender shark that feeds on small schooling fish. Bottom: **Lemon Shark** (*Negaprion brevirostris*). Prized as a delicacy, this small shark has been known to attack swimmers.

Creole Wrasse (*Clepticus parrai*). This wrasse is a spectacularly beautiful purple or violet. Large schools of Creole Wrasses are common in the outer reefs of the Caribbean and adjoining waters. The most prominent coral in this drawing is a **Sea Fan** (*Gorgonia* sp.), a coral, one of a number of related species, with broad, branching, fanlike structures. (Caribbean.)

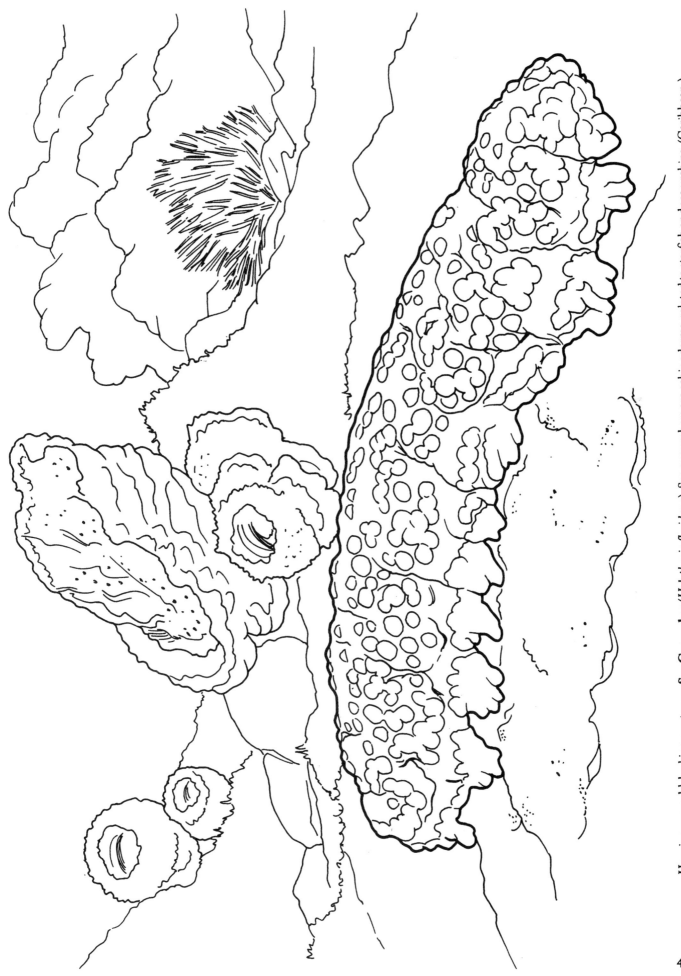

Here is a very odd-looking creature: a **Sea Cucumber** (*Holothuria floridana*). Sea cucumbers are echinoderms, related to starfish and sea urchins. (Caribbean.)

Center: **Atlantic Bottlenose Dolphin** (*Tursiops truncatus*). No sea mammal is as well known or loved as this intelligent, friendly creature, although it is better known to most people from its performances in aquarium shows than from being sighted in the wild. (Caribbean.)

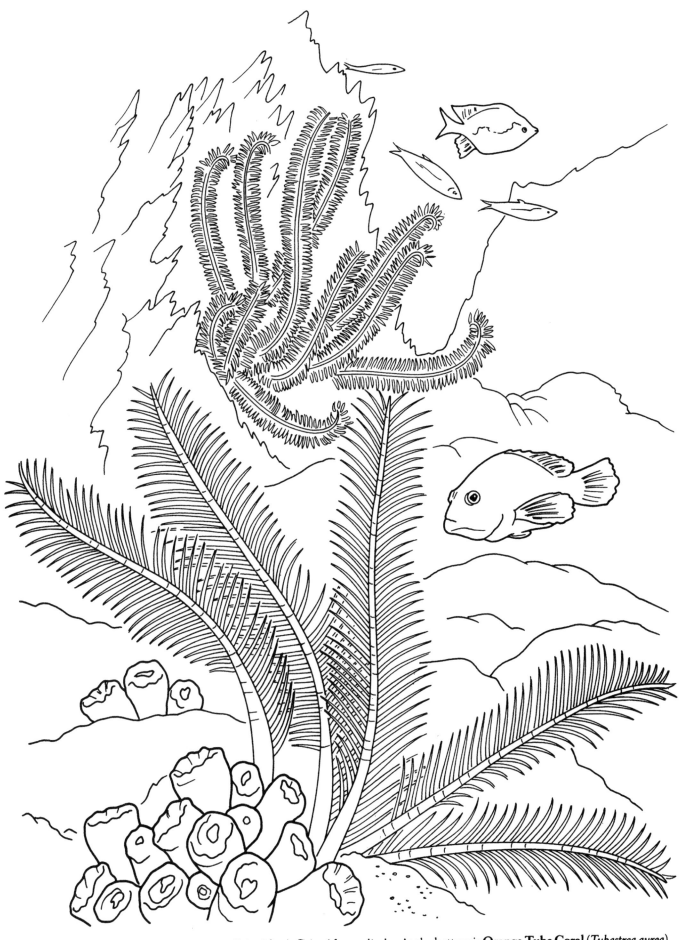

Center: The frilly plantlike creatures are Crinoids. A **Crinoid** (*Nemaster rubiginosa*) is actually a type of starfish with very thin limbs. At the bottom is **Orange Tube Coral** (*Tubastrea aurea*), a type of coral that does not build reefs. (Caribbean.)

The **Queen Angelfish** (*Holocanthus ciliaris*), stately, with a bright blue outline, is a popular aquarium fish. A juvenile swims below. In the foreground is a **Tubular Sponge** (*Verongia longissima*). (Caribbean.)

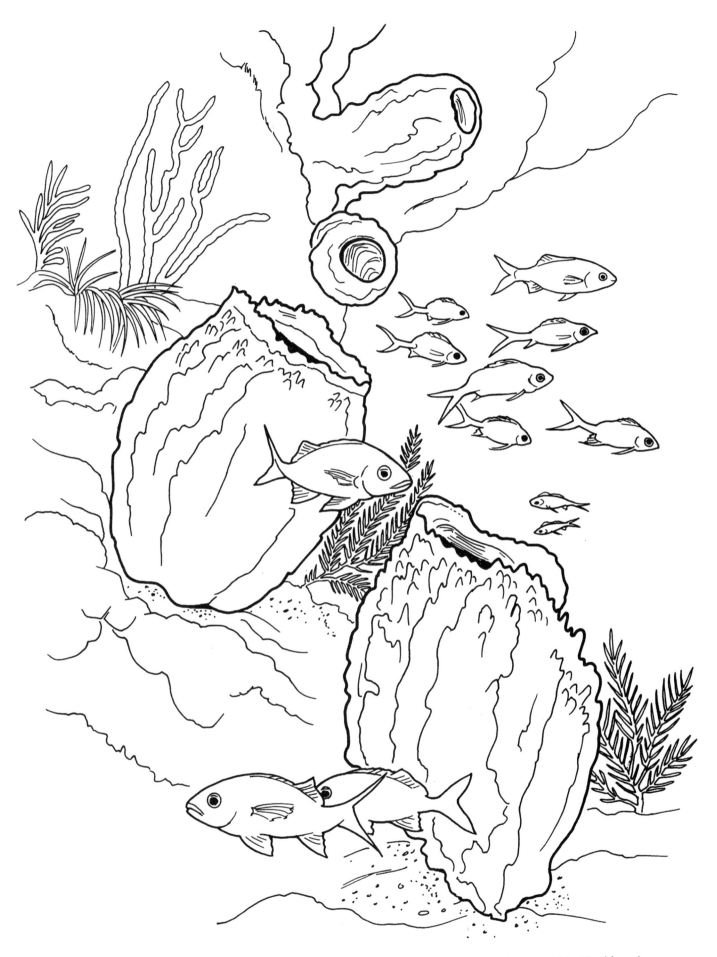

The **Barrel Sponge** (*Xestospongia muta*) is one of the largest sponges, growing to 1.5 meters high. (Caribbean.)

45

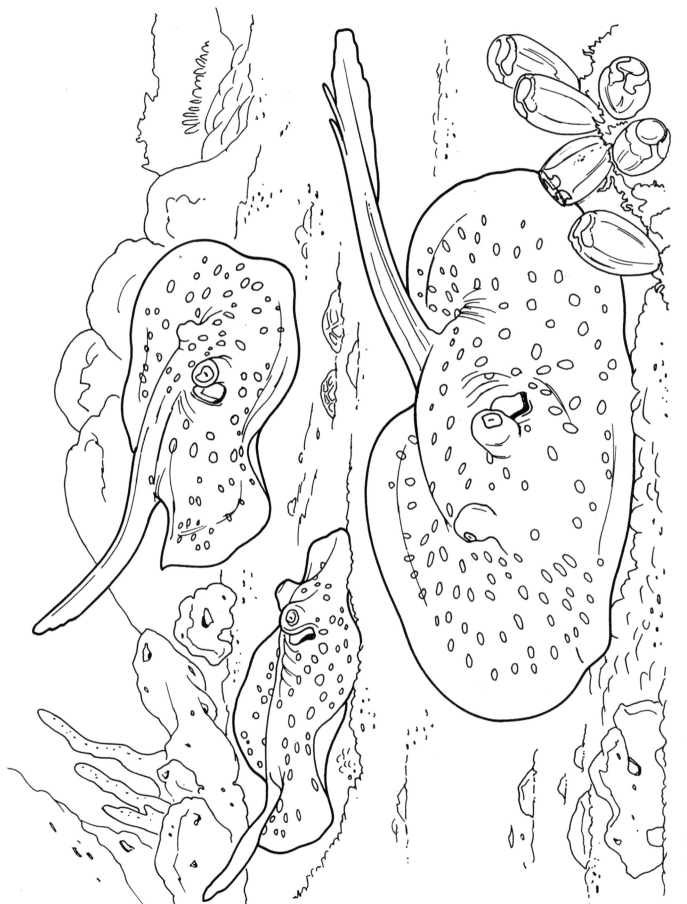

The **Blue-spotted Sting Ray** (*Taeniura lymna*) is a lovely member of its odd family (closely related to sharks), sometimes kept in aquariums. (Caribbean.)

46

Center: **Many-ribbed Hydromedusa** (phylum Cnidaria). This is a jellyfish or polyp similar to those that build corals, except it is free-swimming. In its tentacles is a **Horse-eye Jack** (*Caranx latus*), a schooling fish that feeds on shrimp and other small creatures.

Cottonwick (*Haemulon melanurum*). This small fish, related to the grunts, is seen swimming in a school through a huge reef in the Caribbean.

Seashore Life

Anthony D'Attilio

PUBLISHER'S NOTE

This collection of more than 200 drawings by Anthony D'Attilio is an exciting introduction to the complex and fascinating field of plant and animal marine life. No matter which seashore you live near or visit on vacations, you will probably find some of its inhabitants represented in these pages.

Mr. D'Attilio prepared these drawings carefully and accurately, but in the interest of making the plates as decorative as possible he did allow himself some artistic license. Thus the specimens on any one plate are not necessarily to be found in the same body of water, and occasionally their relative sizes are not strictly correct.

You may be surprised, when you look at the covers of this book, by the wide range of colors and tones nature has subtly intermingled in her marine creatures. You can imitate this natural coloration, or you can use your imagination in selecting colors. The contour lines provided in the drawings can be used as guidelines for the subtle blending of colors, as in nature, or as sharp demarcation lines between areas of flat color, if your aim is more decorative. Whichever method you choose, enjoy coloring and creating for yourself either true-to-life depictions of marine plants and animals, or more fanciful creatures for framing or collages.

The varied specimens in this collection represent some of the most common and some of the most exotic forms of sea life in the oceans of the world. We hope these drawings and the identifications of the creatures will lead you to a deeper interest in this mysterious and still explorable area. You may then want to consult the more detailed field guides to marine life in your own area.

1. Clown anemone fish   2. Orange anemone   3. Wentletrap
4. Sea biscuit urchin

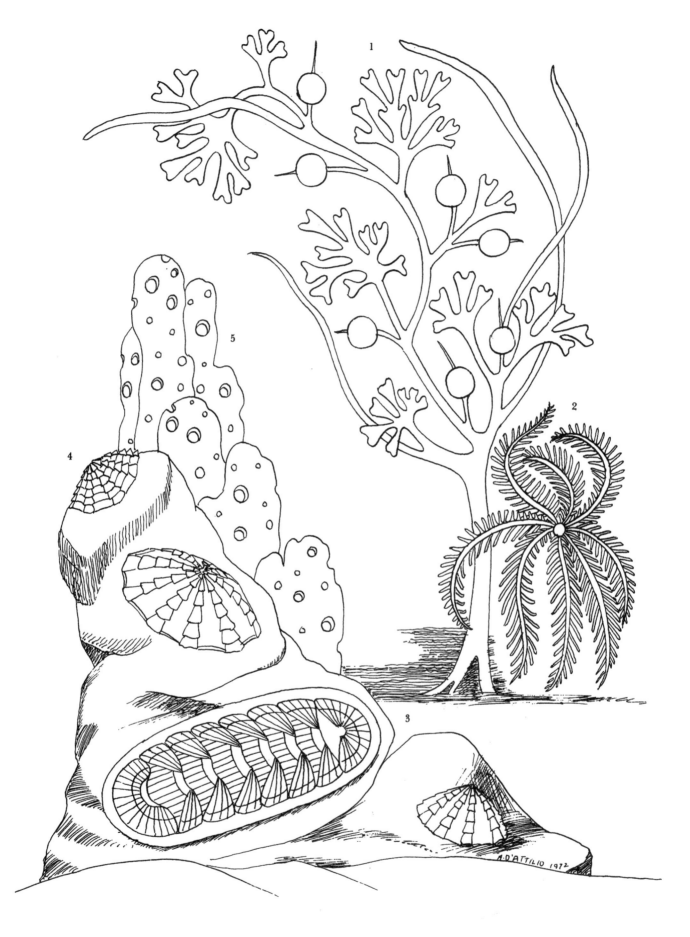

1. Berry seaweed 2. Feather star 3. Chiton 4. Limpets
5. Stony coral

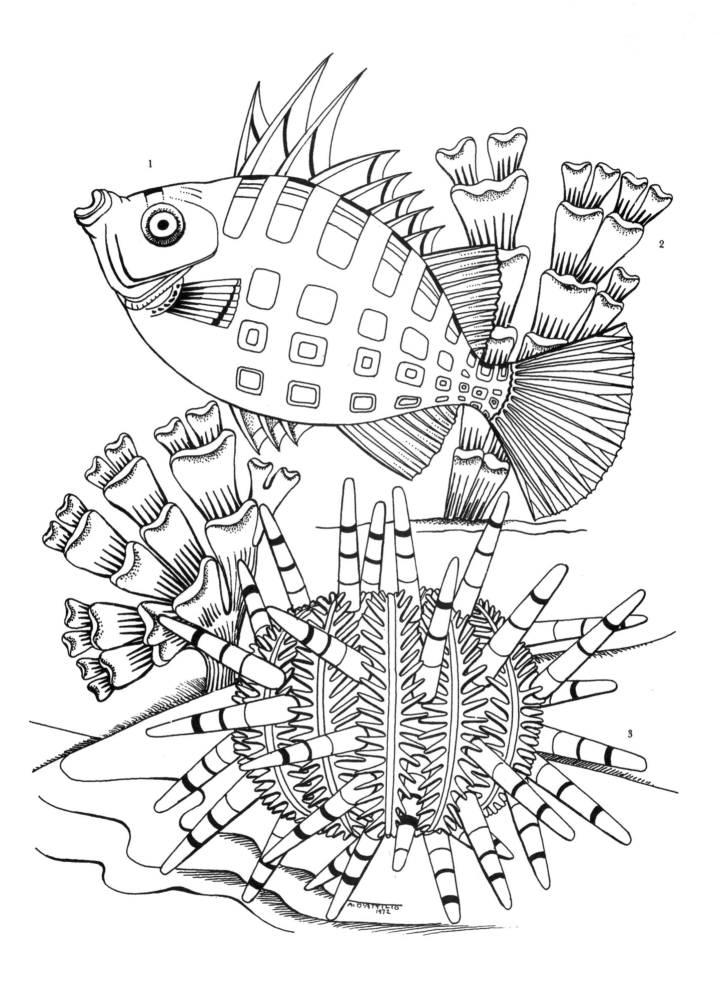

1. Porgy   2. Coral algae   3. Club-spined sea urchin

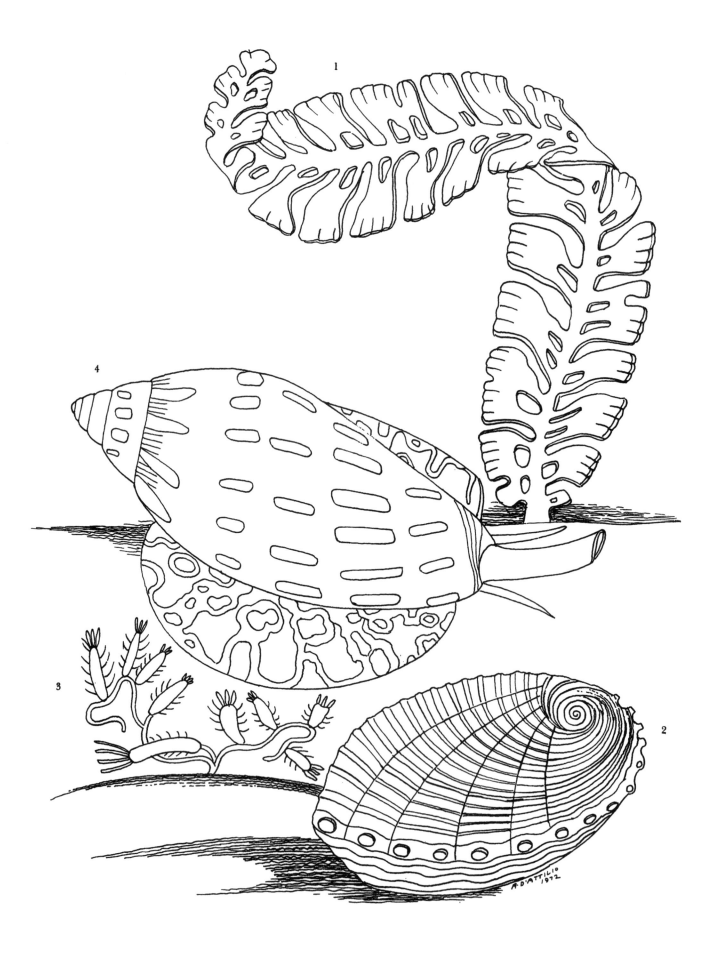

1. Kelp   2. Abalone shell   3. Branching crest animal   4. Volute

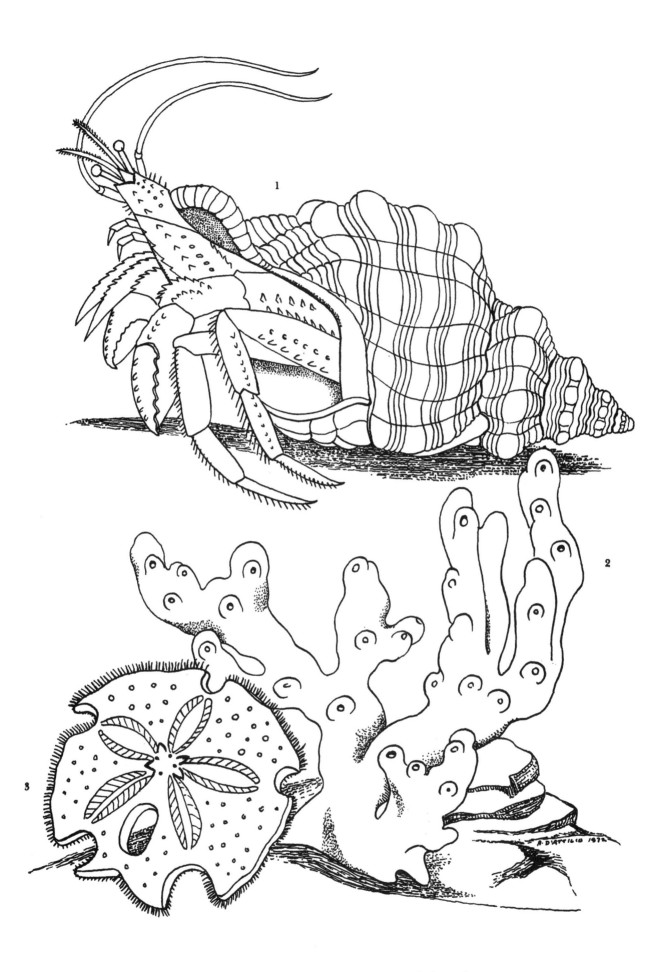

1. Tulip shell with Hermit crab   2. Branching hydrocoral
3. Keyhole urchin

1. Hydromedusan jellyfish 2. Eyed coral
3. Sponge 4. Scallop 5. Spiny starfish 6. Sea squirts

1. Sea slug   2. Red seaweed   3. Sessile jellyfish
4. Scorpion fish   5. Alaria seaweed

1

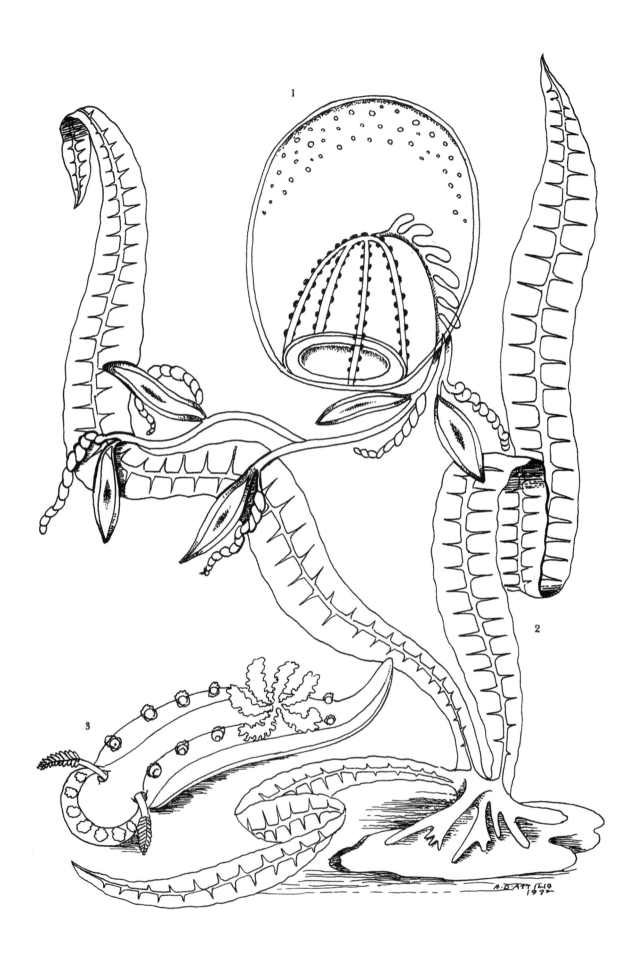

3

2

58   1. Bladder jellyfish 2. Kelp 3. Sea slug

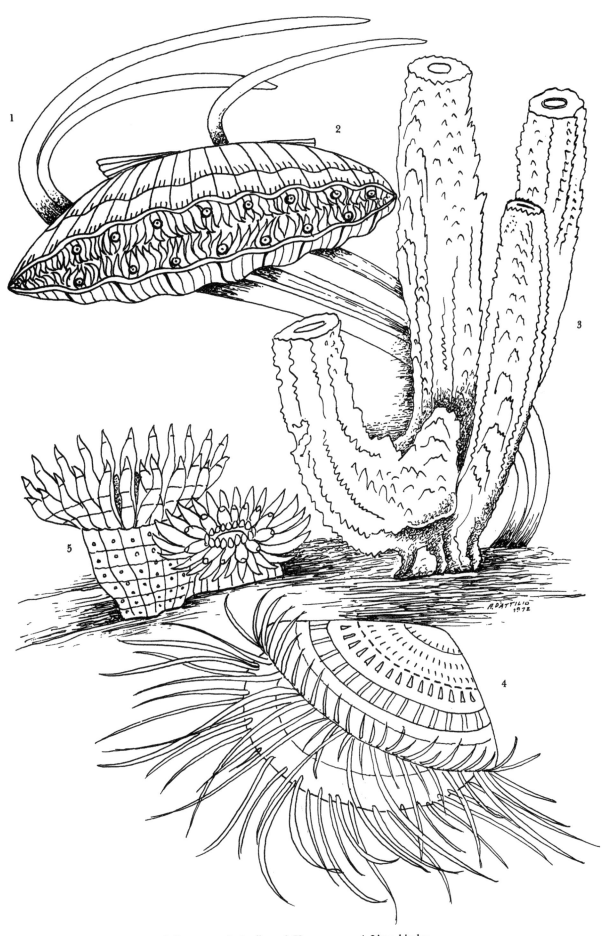

1. Sea grass   2. Scallop   3. Vase sponge   4. Lima bivalve
5. Blue anemone

1. Ivory shell   2. Sponge   3. Volva   4. Seaweed   5. Murex shell

1. Brown blister weed   2. Ghost shrimp   3. Fig shell
4. Fargo's worm shell   5. Abalone shell   6. Rock barnacles

1. Oval ring weed 2. Sea squirts 3. Denuded sea urchin

1. Bubble shell   2. Saddleback butterfly fish
3. Clustering anemone   4. Gemmed anemone

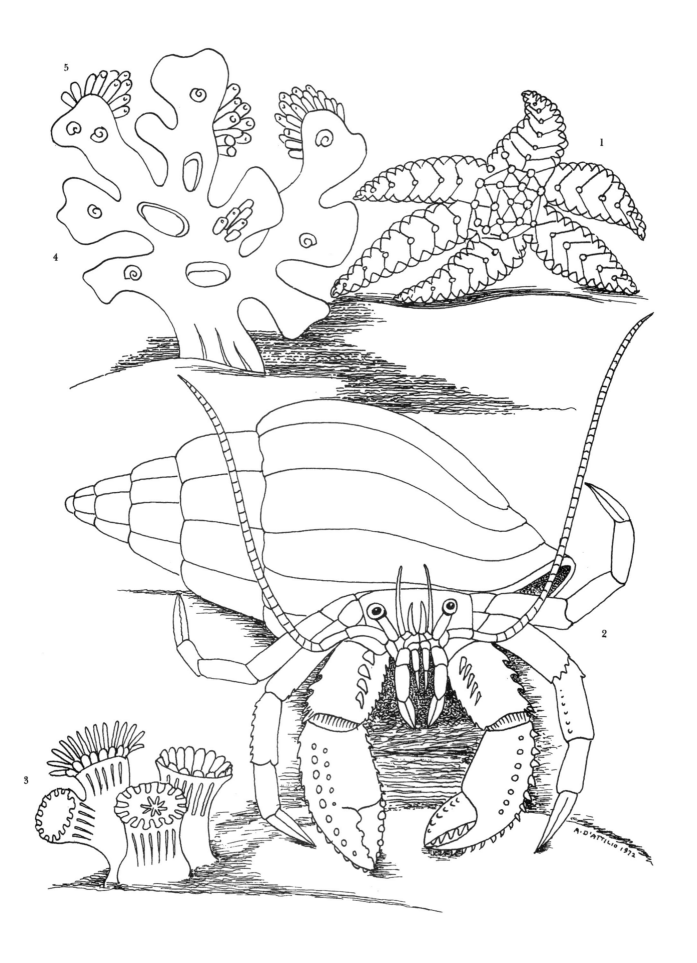

1. Common sea star   2. Hermit crab inhabiting Gastropod shell
3. Astrangia coral   4. Irish moss   5. Egg cases of shell animals

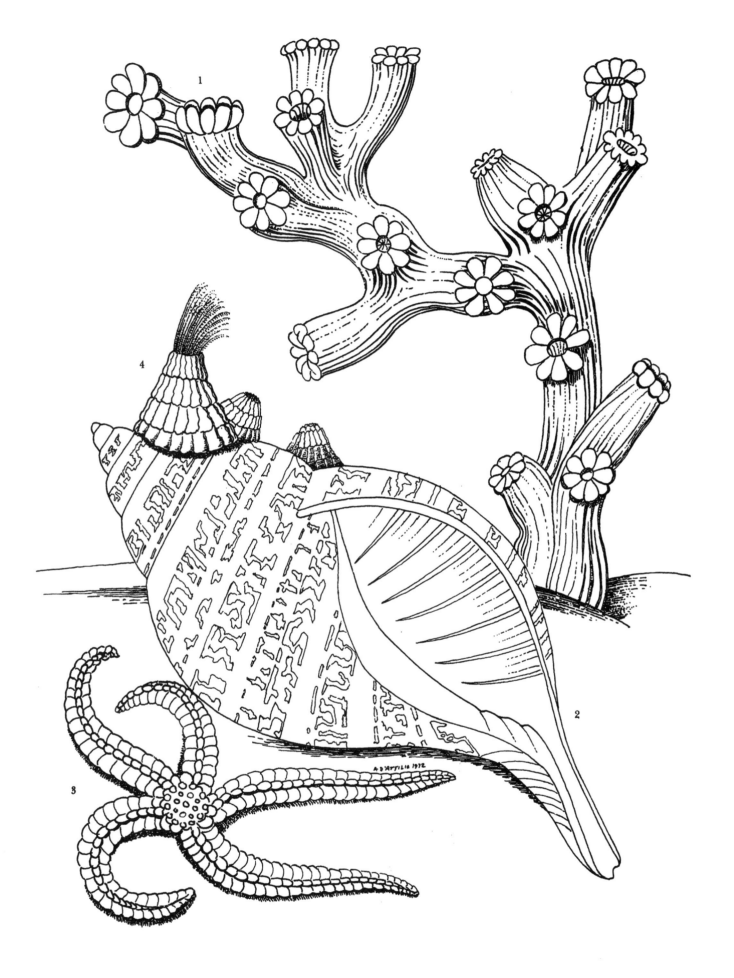

1. Branching coral 2. Tulip shell 3. Long-armed starfish
4. Rock barnacles

1. Triggerfish 2. Green soft coral 3. Bread-crumb sponge
4. Astrangia coral

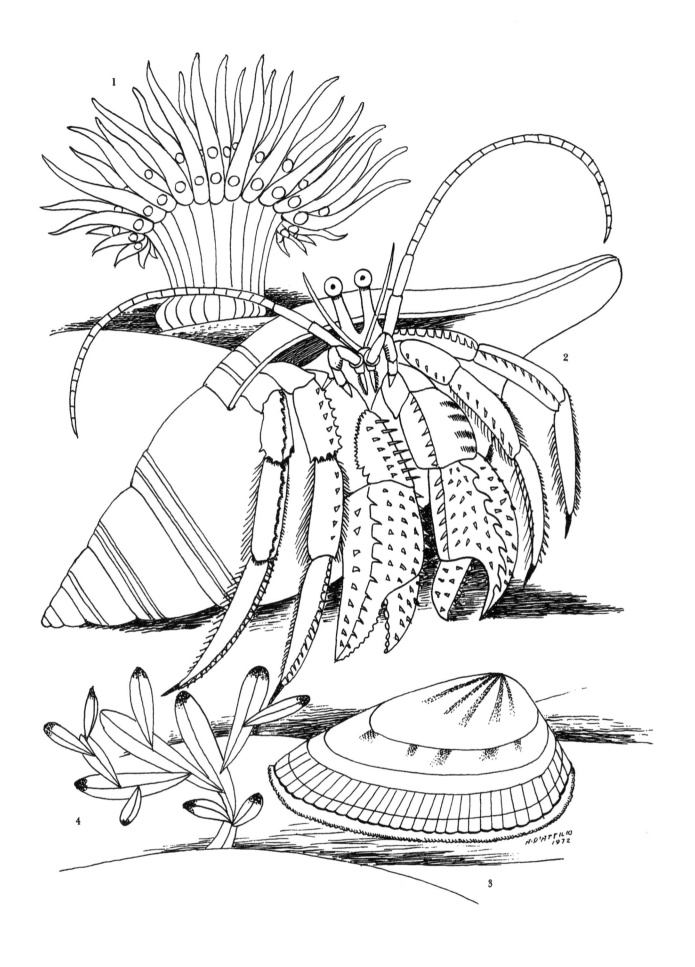

1. Sagartia anemone
2. Soldier hermit crab inhabiting Gastropod shell
3. Venus bivalve   4. Club seaweed

67

1. Fan worm in tube 2. Sea squirt 3. Rock barnacles
4. Ochre sea star 5. Seaweed 6. Turbo shell
7. Cup sponge 8. Hydroids

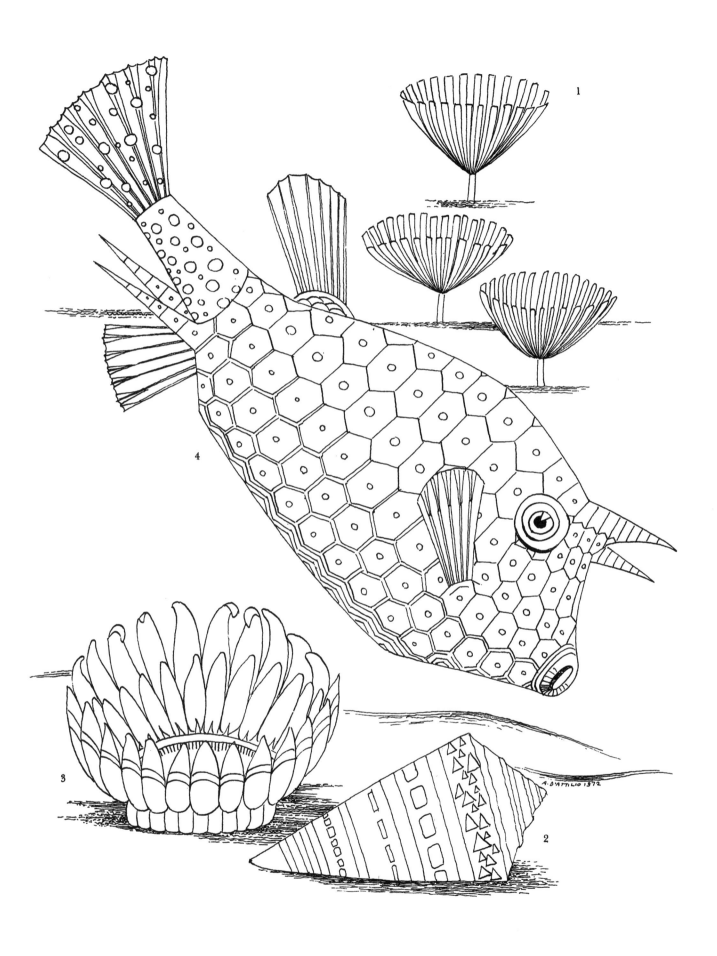

1. Sea daisies   2. Cone shell   3. Dahlia anemone
4. Cowfish

1. Long-nosed butterfly fish   2. Fan seaweed
3. Livona shell   4. Sea star

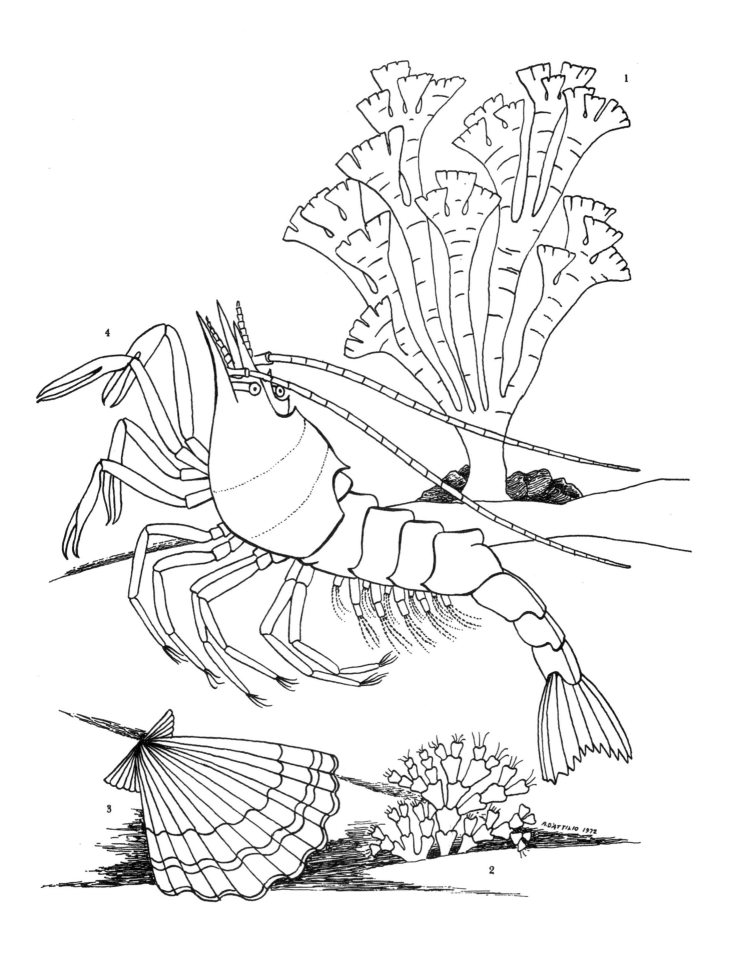

1. Green branching fan weed   2. Stony algae   3. Scallop
4. Spiny lobster

73

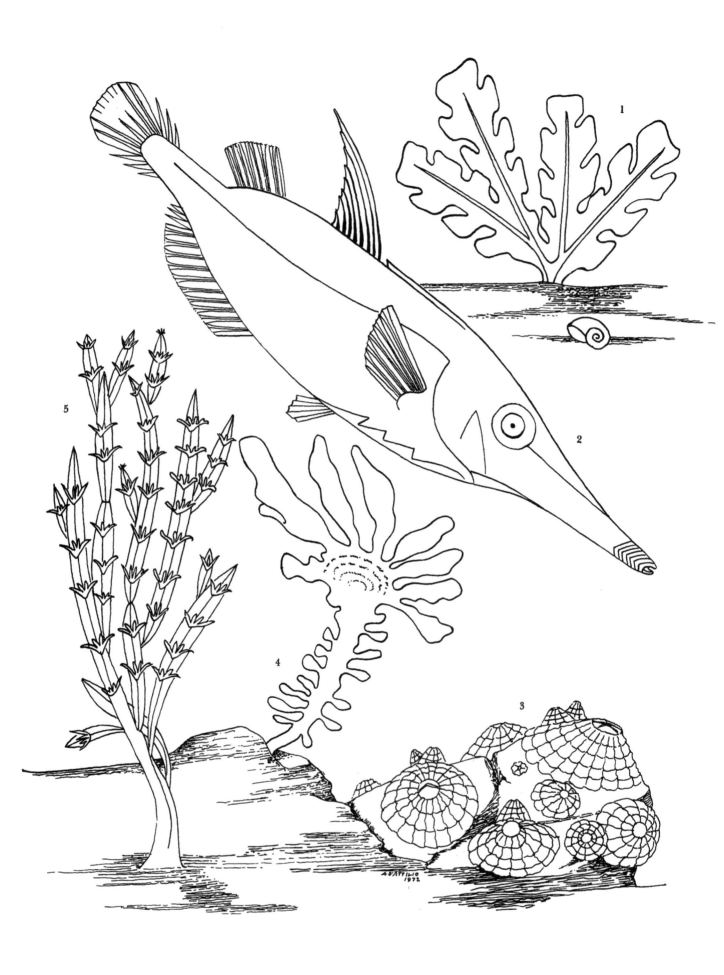

1. Palm seaweed   2. Long-nosed snook   3. Rock barnacles
4. Rocky pool green weed   5. Sea whip

1. Branching sponge   2. Brittle sea star   3. Turbo shell
4. Sand dollar

1. Fringed Australian reef sea horse   2. Spotted snail
3. Burrowing shrimp   4. Brain coral

1. Mussels   2. Black-tip orange seaweed   3. Limpet
4. Plumed sea slug   5. Cancer crab   6. Goose barnacle

1. Leaflike flatworm   2. Common Easter sea star
3. Tellina shell   4. Gigartina seaweed

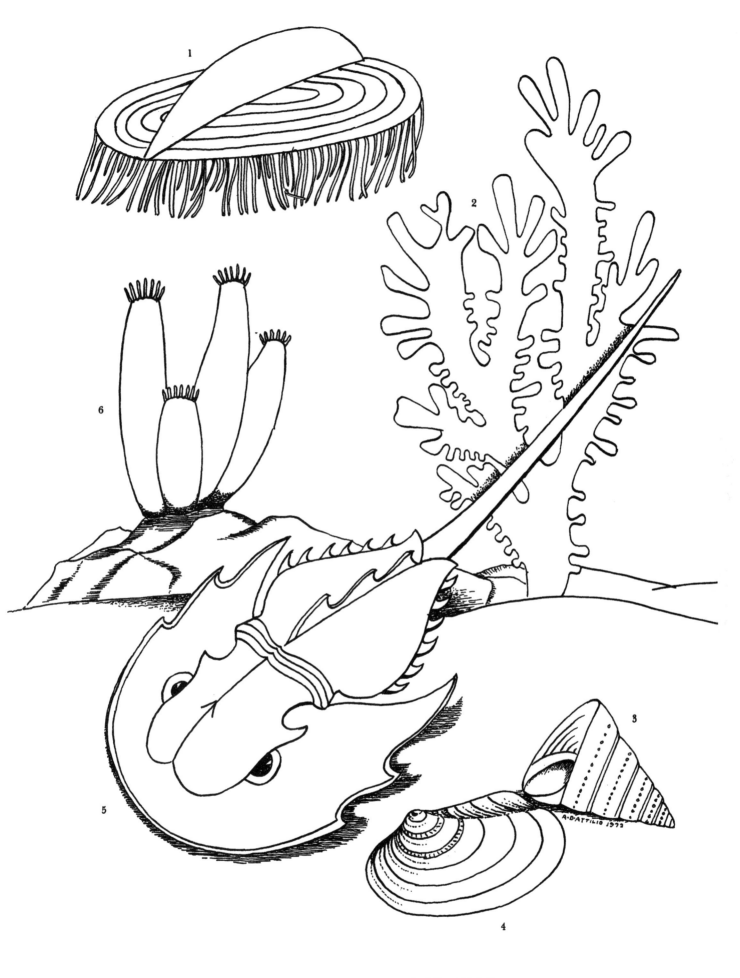

1. Vellela jellyfish 2. Alaria seaweed 3. Trochid shell
4. Bivalve shell 5. Horseshoe crab 6. Lime sponge

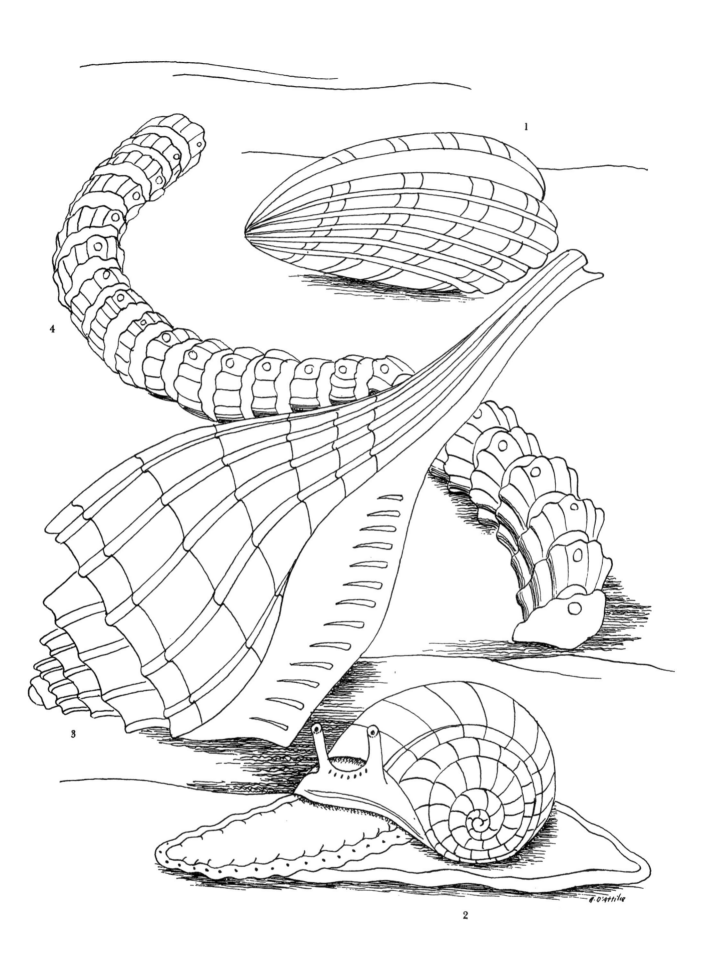

1. Mussel   2. Shark-eye Polynices shell   3. Whelk
4. Whelk egg case

1. Japanese sea horse 2. Staghorn coral 3. Sponge
4. Short-legged crab

1. Purple fantip seaweed 2. Yellow sponge 3. Limpet
4. Calico crab

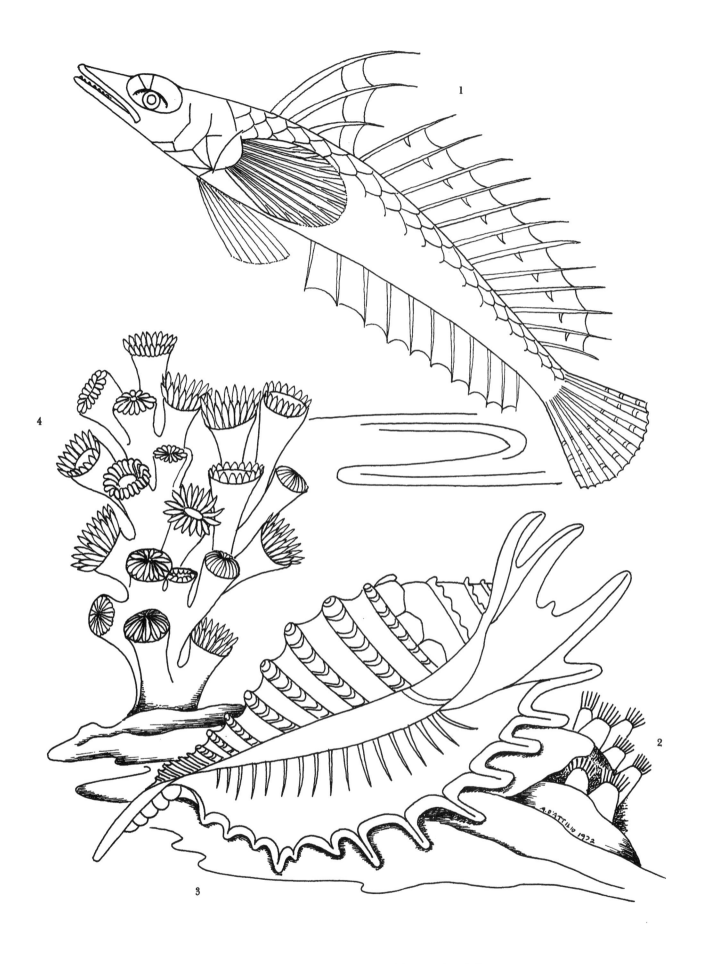

1. Spiny sea fish   2. Sponges   3. Violet scorpion shell
4. Astrangia coral

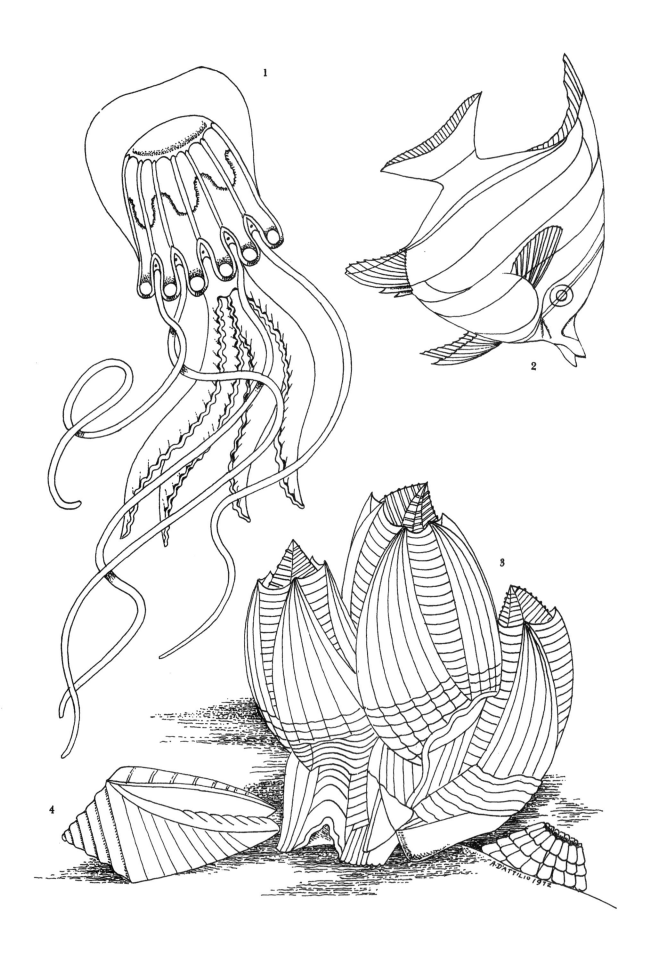

1. Jellyfish   2. Angelfish   3. Rock barnacles
4. Cone shell

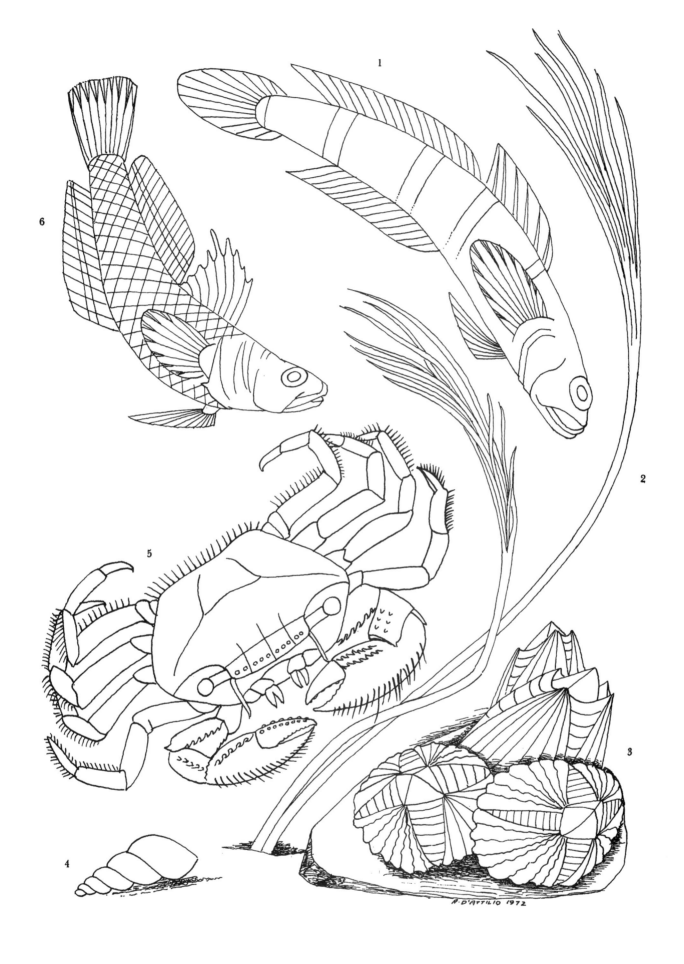

1. Goby   2. Kelp   3. Rock barnacles   4. Pheasant shell
5. Swimming crab   6. Blenny

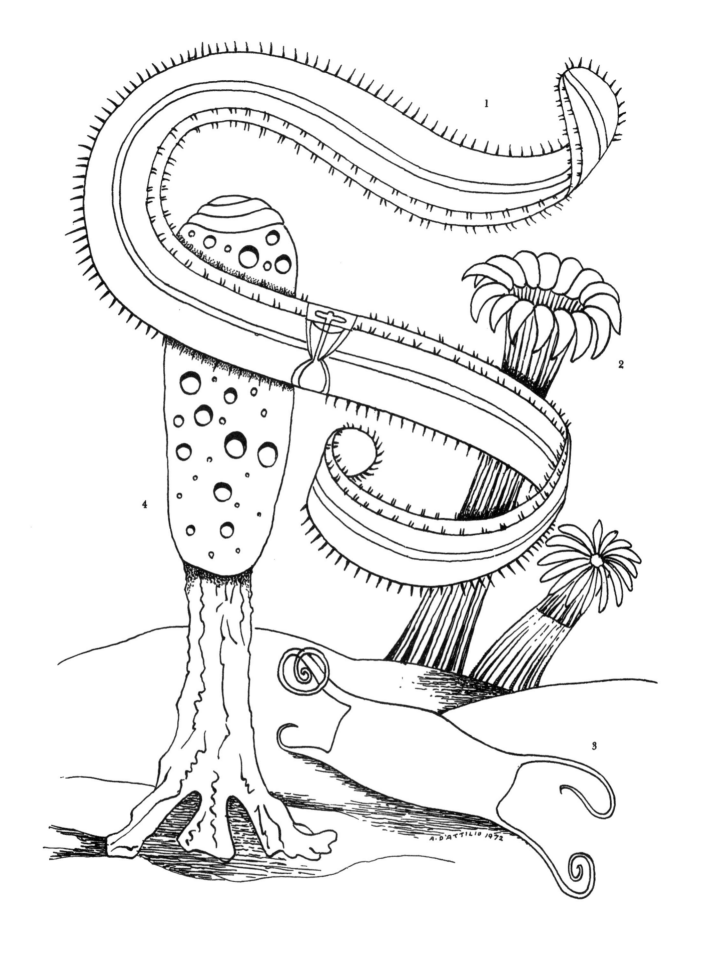

1. Comb jellyfish   2. Zooanthid anemone
3. Sea skate egg case (Sea purse)   4. Column sponge

1. Moonfish   2. Orange anemone   3. Sand dollar
4. Purple sea fan   5. Green seaweed

1

A. D'ATTILIO 1972

2

1. Atlantic sea horses   2. Sea grass

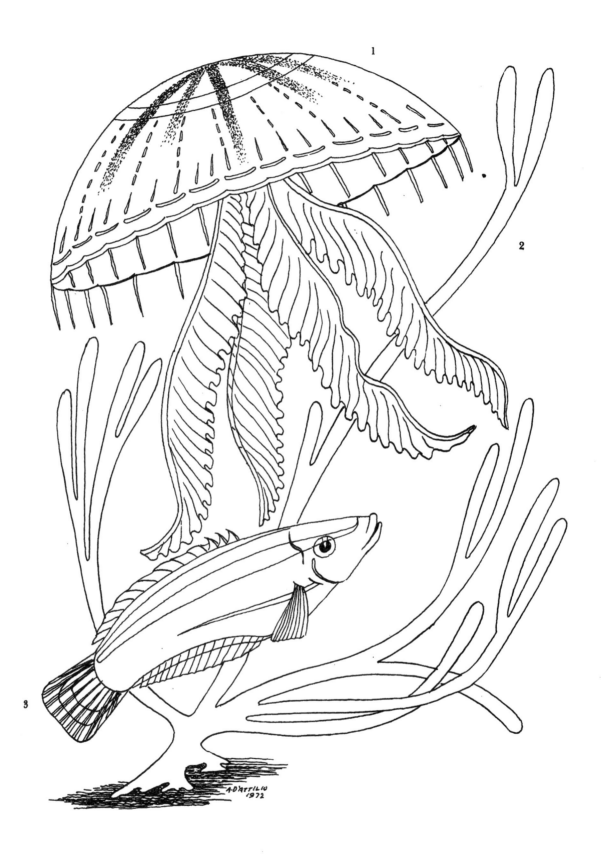

1. Moon jellyfish   2. Sea whip   3. Emperor fish

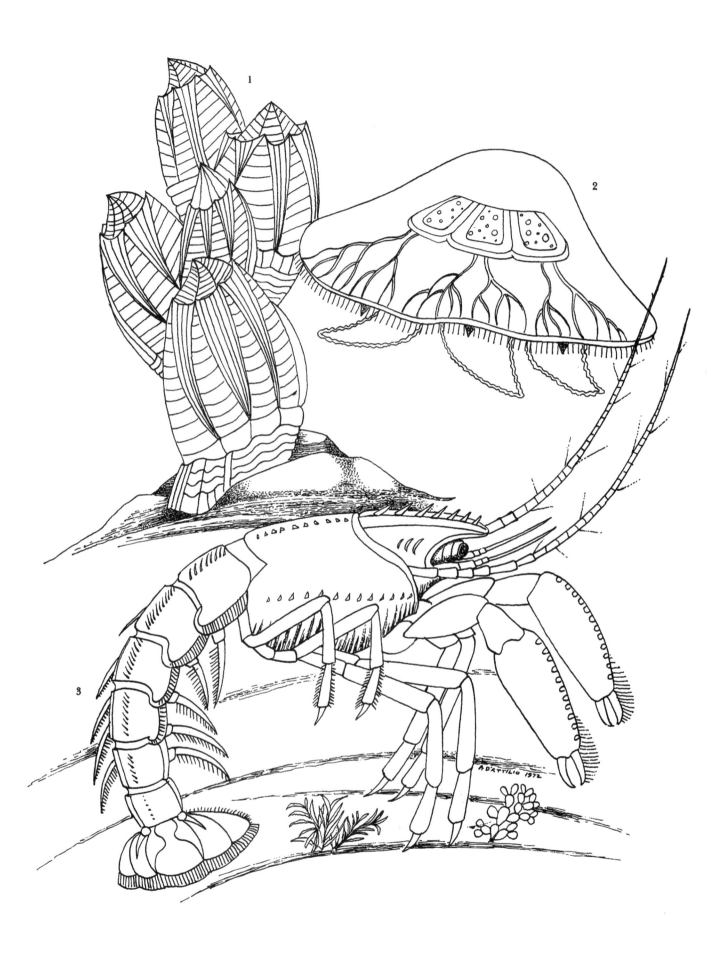

1. Rock barnacles 2. Aurelia jellyfish 3. Prawn

1. Snapper   2. Staghorn coral
3. Stony mushroom coral   4. Cowry

1. Small rock cod   2. Dead man's fingers sponge
3. Spotted siphonalia   4. Stony branching coral
5. Sundial shell

1. Mediterranean cuttlefish   2. Stony algae
3. Strombus shell   4. Mexican chiton   5. Rock barnacles

1. Hydroids   2. Wrasse   3. Coralline   4. Top shell
5. Blue sea star   6. Madreporarian orange reef coral

1. Red seaweed   2. Harp shell   3. Blue and green coral
4. West Australian volute

1. Pipefish 2. Young sea horse
3. Blue coral showing polyps 4. Sea whip

Shells of
the World

Lucia de Leiris

Publisher's Note

In countless collections around the world, strung on necklaces or scattered on the beach, the colorful patterns and intricate shapes of shells enchant and amaze us. And yet, shells are merely the homes of the master builders and craftsmen of the animal world, the mollusks. Except for the Acorn Barnacle (which zoologists place in the Arthropod phylum), all of the shell species illustrated in this book are soft-bodied, gilled invertebrates belonging to the Mollusca phylum, a group that also includes such nonshelled marine animals as the octopus and squid and the land-based snails and garden slug. Shelled mollusks are found most abundantly burrowing in sandy bottoms or clinging to rocks and reefs in temperate and tropical waters, but some species inhabit deep ocean trenches and frigid arctic coasts. Shielded from predators and harsh environments by their protective shells, mollusks flourish as herbivores, carnivorous hunters, scavengers, parasites or strainers of nutrient-laden sea water.

Although the shape of the soft body in the shell varies from species to species, the majority of mollusks have a wedge-shaped "foot" which can poke through a shell opening and push the shell along a sea bottom. All of the mollusks have a layer of flesh close to the inside of the shell, and it is this "mantle" that builds the shell, ring by ring. Sometimes as colorful as the shell itself, the mantle of such species as the cowries can extend from inside to cover the outside of the shell. To create the dots, bands and streaks on the shell, glands in the mantle mix color pigments with the calcium carbonate substance that forms the shell. As the animals grows to maturity, more of the secreted material is added around the edges of the shell opening. Through this process, mollusks add spines, spires, whorls and knobs and create fantastic shell exteriors like those seen on the Spiny Murex and Trumpet Triton.

This book includes many remarkable mollusks. The Violet Sea Snail begins life as a male and later changes to a female, floats on the ocean's surface with the help of bubbles, and douses its prey with purple dye before eating it. The Rough Lima entangles attackers in sticky tentacle threads which it also uses to build nests and latch onto rocks. The Chambered Nautilus, a mollusk with an ancient lineage, is more closely related to the seventy-foot-long Giant Squid than to snails and clams its own size. The Atlantic Bay Scallop has many bright blue eyes dotting its mantle and uses jet propulsion to dodge away from enemies in a zigzag motion. The Textile Cone possesses a poisonous sting that can kill predatory octopi and careless humans, and the Striate Cone harpoons, paralyzes and swallows fish.

Many of the shells pictured inside are widely used and highly valued by mankind. In the past, cowries and clams have served as money in Africa, Asia and the Americas. The deep, booming sound that can be attained by blowing on Trumpet Tritons have made them popular in official ceremonies. Bull-Mouth Helmet shells are an important source of material for carving small portraits in cameo jewelry. Some shells, such as the Golden Cowry and Emperor's Slit Shell, are highly prized by collectors today, and in eighteenth-century Europe a close relative of the Pallas Wentletrap was worth more than the finest gemstone. Through the ages mollusks have supplied men with purple dyes for royal robes, pearls and polished shells for decoration, and wish scallop, mussel and clam meat for the dinner table; indeed, in some places large clam shells are used as dinner plates.

The forty-five illustrations in the *Shells of the World* coloring pages provide you with the pleasant task of recreating the world of nature's own painters and sculptors. Captions are provided with each illustration listing the common and scientific names of the species shown, the average length of the mature animal, and the area of the world which the shells inhabit. In certain cases the extension of the mantle over the shell has been noted. Perhaps these drawings will inspire you to learn more about shells: about mussels that can melt rocks, teredo worms that eat ships and carrier shells that are themselves collectors of shells. But for now, dive inside and discover the world of shells—on coral reefs, among sponges and seaweed on an ocean floor or under a palm tree on a wave-beaten shore.

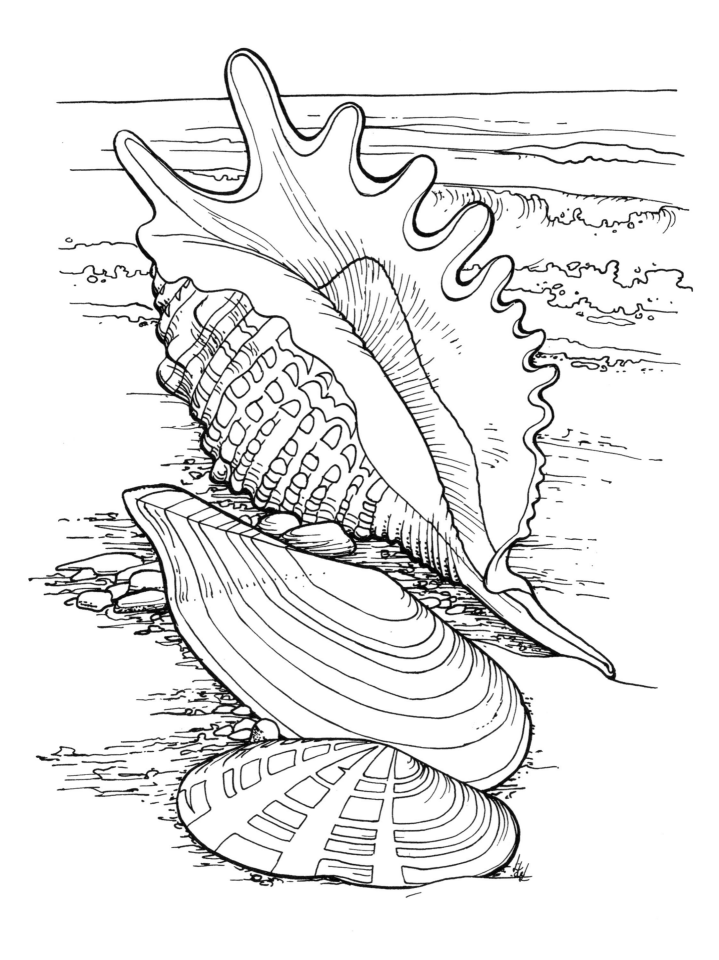

TOP TO BOTTOM: Violet Spider Conch (*Lambis violacea*), 4″; Perrier's Tellin (*Tellina perrieri*), 3″; Jackknife Clam (*Siliqua radiata*), 1.5″. Indo-Pacific area.

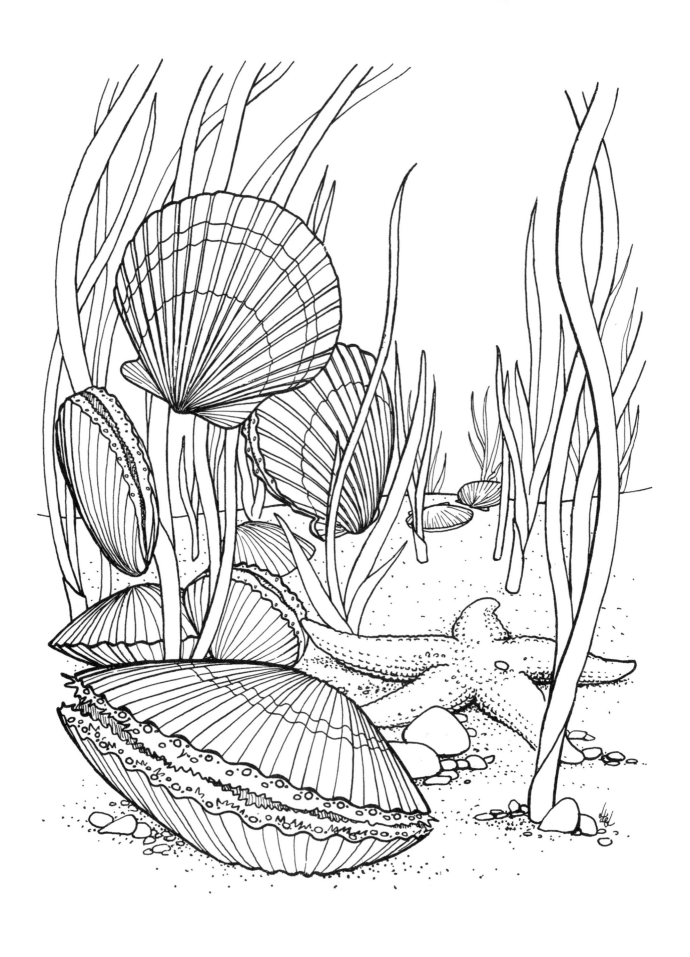

Atlantic Bay Scallops (*Aequipecten irradians*), 3″, swimming away from predatory starfish. New England.

BOTTOM: **Blue Mussels** (*Mytilus edulis*), 3″. RIGHT MIDDLE: **Waved Whelk** (*Buccinum undatum*), 4″. New England.

TOP LEFT: Lion's Paw (*Lyropecten nodosus*), 4″. TOP RIGHT: Sentis Scallops (*Chlamys sentis*), 1″. MIDDLE: Banded Tulip (*Fasciolaria distans*), 3″. BOTTOM: Cabrit's Murex (*Murex cabriti*), 3″. Florida and Caribbean area.

BOTTOM TO TOP: Butterfly Moons (*Naticarius alapapilionis*), 1″; Cardinal Miter (*Mitra cardinalis*), 2″; Episcopal Miter (*Mitra mitra*), 5″. Indo-Pacific area.

TOP TO BOTTOM: Fighting Stromb [Conch] (*Strombus pugilis*), 5″; **Turkey Wing** (*Arca zebra*), 3″; **Coquina shells** (*Donax variabilis*), 0.8″. Florida and Caribbean area.

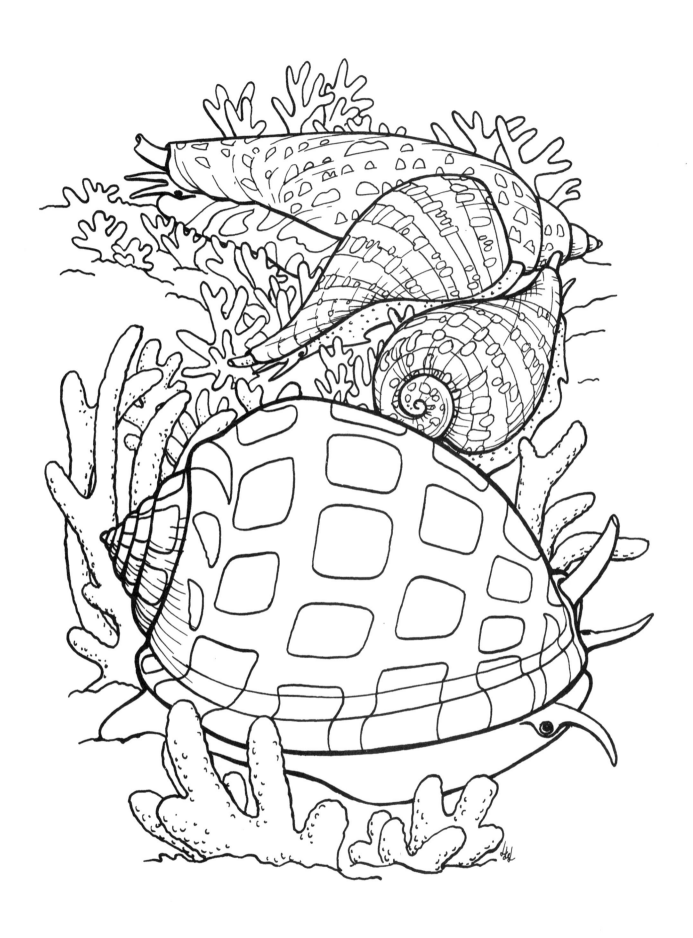

TOP TO BOTTOM: Gross's Volute (*Volutoconus grossi*), 6.7"; Fig Shells (*Ficus subintermedia*), 3.2"; Areole Helmet (*Phalium areola*), 3.5". Australia.

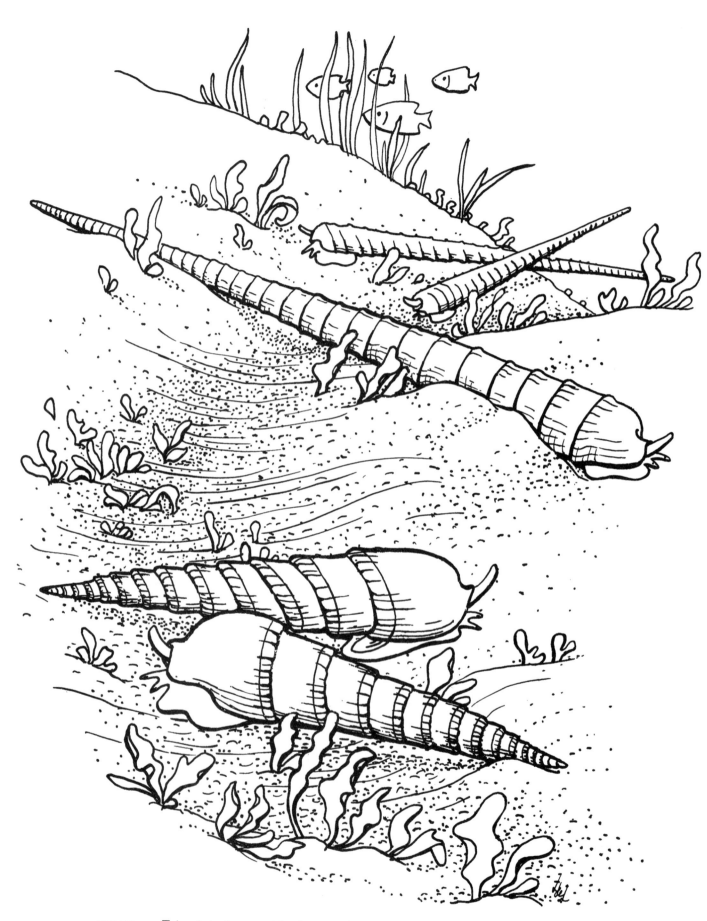

TOP THREE: Triseriate Augers (*Terebra triseriata*), 4.3″. BOTTOM TWO: White-Edged Augers (*Terebra albomarginata*), 2.8″. Australia.

Wiseman's Volute (*Cymbiolacca wisemani*), 3.2″. Australia.

Helicina Margarite (*Margarites helicinus*), 0.3″. Canada.

TOP TWO (SIDE BY SIDE): Venus Cowries (*Cypraea venusta*), 3.2″, with mantle retracted (left) and extended (right). THREE (SMALL) ON RIGHT: Saul's Cowries (*Cypraea saulae*), 1.2″, with mantle retracted (top) and extended (middle) and an empty shell. BOTTOM TWO: Sieve Cowries (*Cypraea cribraria*), 1.4″, with mantle retracted (right) and extended (left). LEFT CENTER: Map Cowry (*Cypraea mappa*), 3.2″, with mantle retracted. Australia.

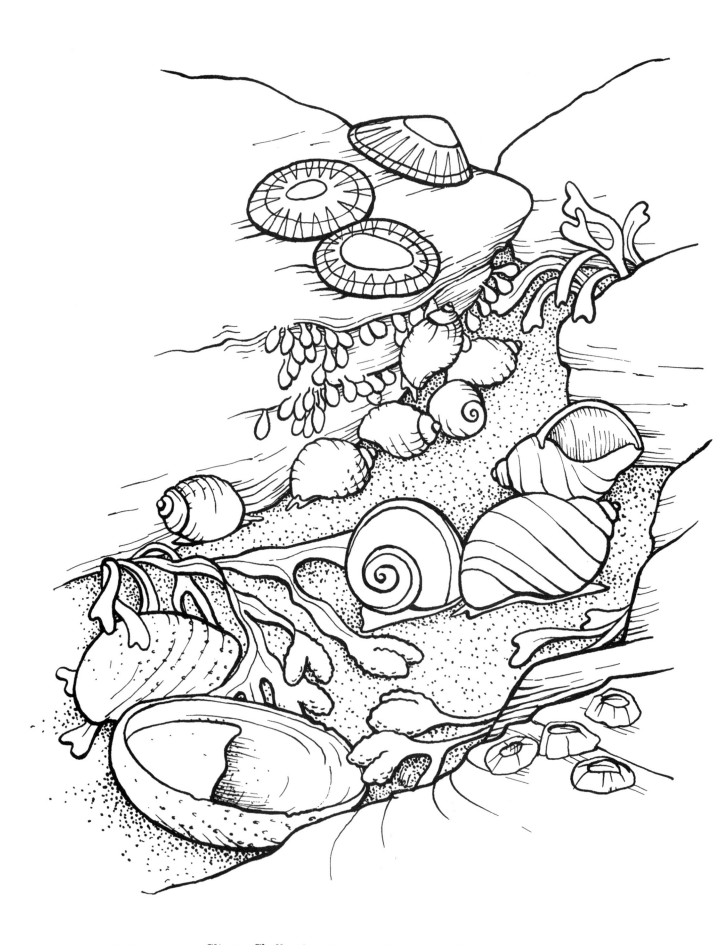

BOTTOM TO TOP: Slipper Shells (*Crepidula fornicata*), 1.5″; Dogwinkles (*Thais lapillus*), 1.5″; Dog Whelks with egg capsules (*Nassarius vibex*), .5″; Tortoiseshell Limpets (*Acmaea testudinalis*), 1″. New England.

110

COUNTERCLOCKWISE FROM TOP: A young Fluted Giant Clam (*Tridacna squamosa*), adult 12″;
Spindle Tibia (*Tibia fusus*), 12″; Martini's Tibia (*Tibia martinii*), 6″; Auger Turritella
(*Turritella terebra*), 4″; Miter Shell (*Mitra vittata*), 2.5″; Subulate Auger (*Terebra subulata*),
5″. Indo-Pacific area.

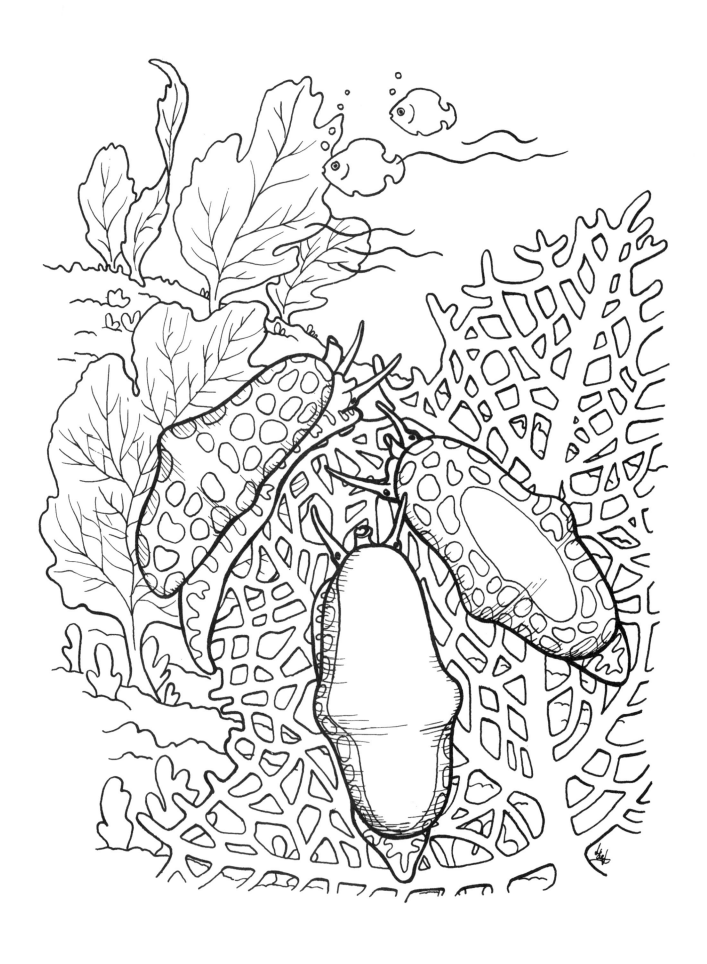

Flamingo Tongues (*Cyphoma gibbosum*), 1″, living on sea fans with mantle fully and partially extended over shell. Florida and Caribbean area.

Trumpet Tritons (*Charonia variegata*), 15″, eating sea urchins. Florida and Caribbean area.

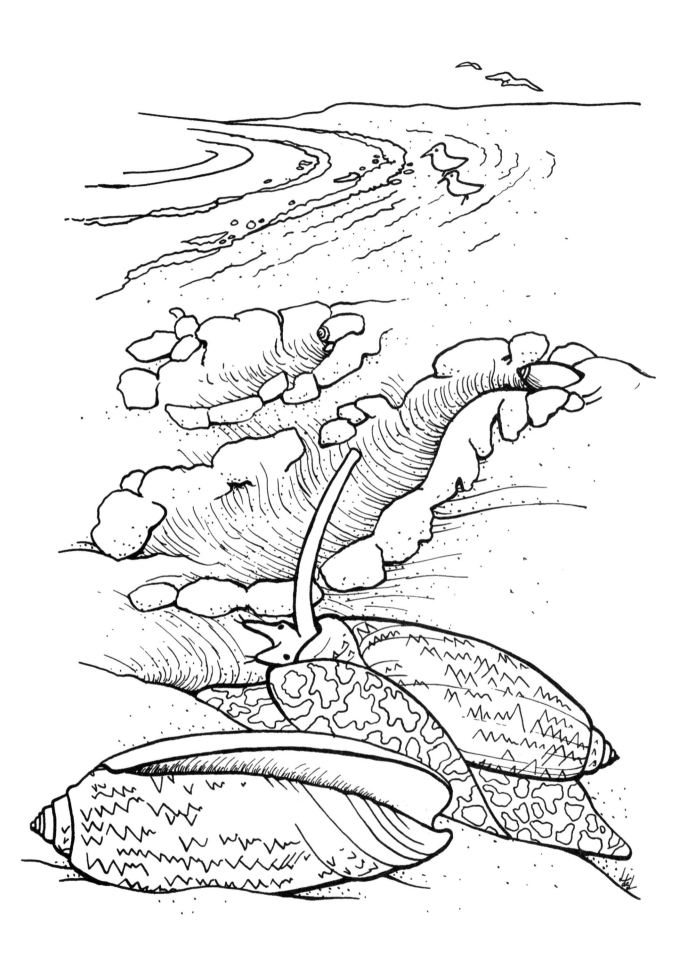

Lettered Olives (*Oliva sayana*), 2.5″, burrowing in sand. Florida and Caribbean area.

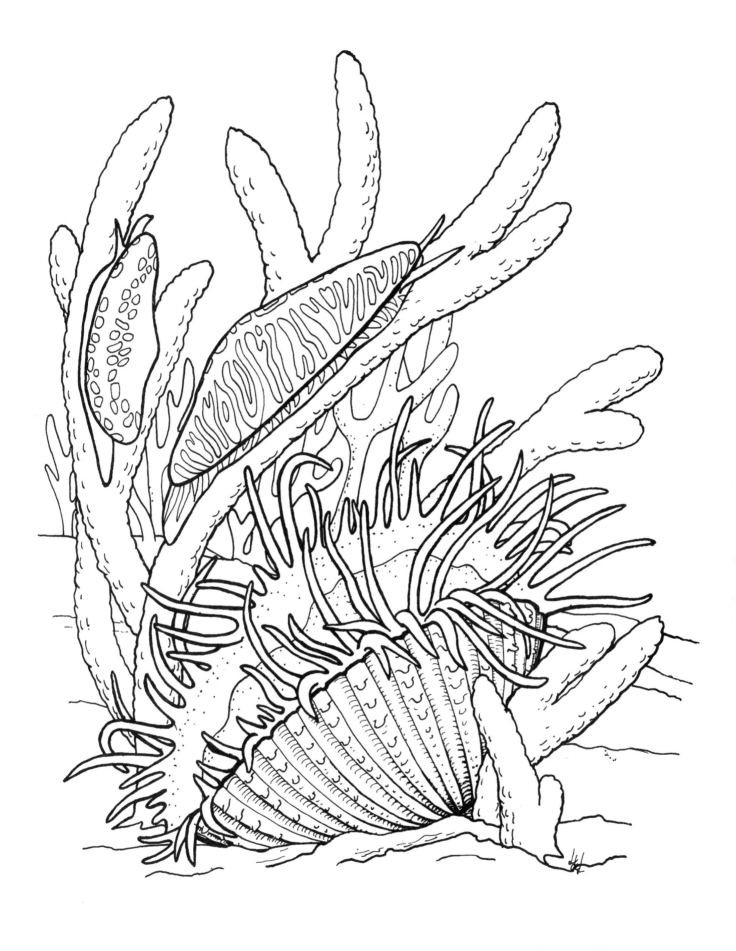

TOP TO BOTTOM: McGinty's Cyphoma (*Cyphoma mcgintyi*), 1″, with mantle extended; Fingerprint Cyphoma (*Cyphoma signatum*), 1″, with mantle extended; Rough Lima (*Lima scabra*), 2″. Florida and Caribbean area.

TOP TO BOTTOM: **Periwinkle** (*Littorina littorea*), 1.2″; **Acorn Barnacles** (*Balanus balanoides*), 0.4″; **Dove Shell** (*Anachis avara*), 0.4″. New England.

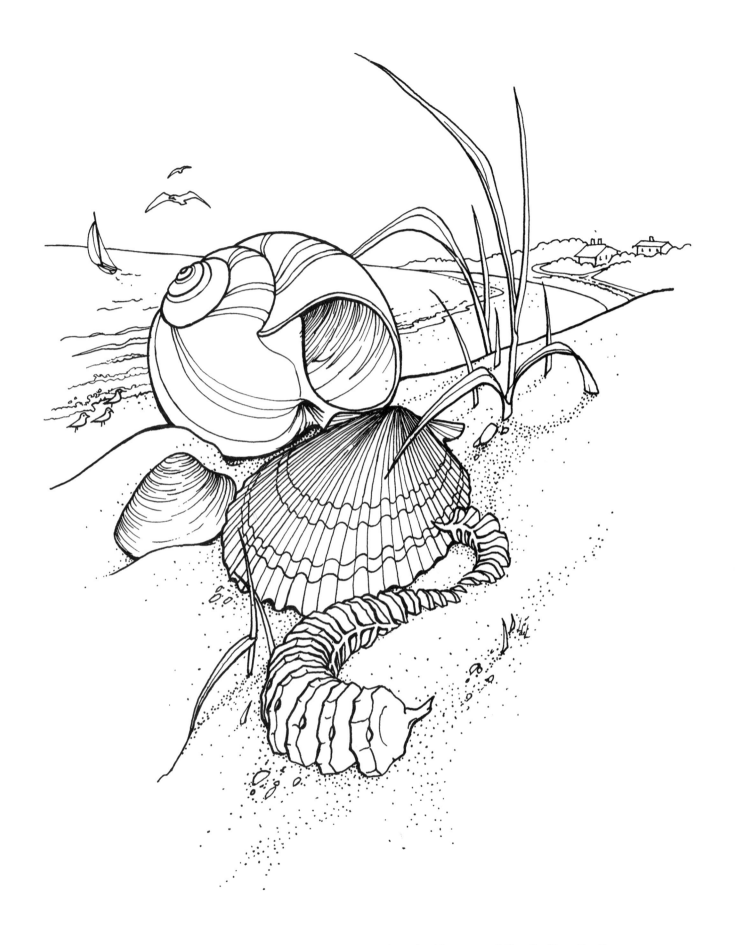

TOP: Common Northern Moon Snail (*Lunatia heros*), 4″. RIGHT: Atlantic Bay Scallop (*Aequipecten irradians*), 3″. LEFT: A young Atlantic Surf Clam (*Spisula solidissima*), adult 6″. BOTTOM: Whelk egg case (*Busycon*). New England.

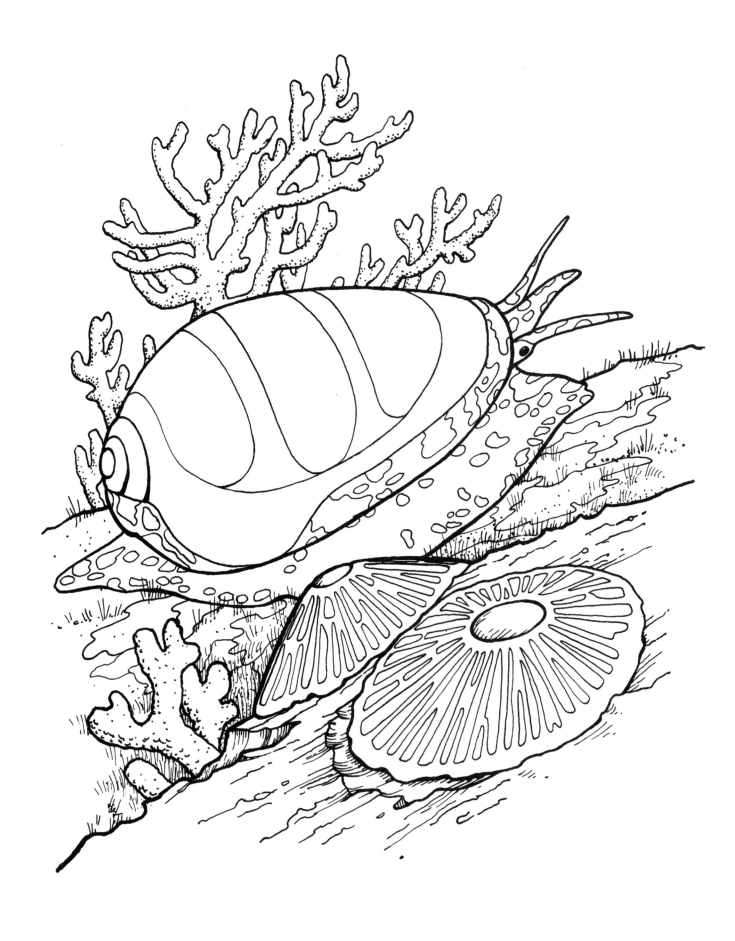

TOP TO BOTTOM: Orange Marginella (*Prunum carneum*), 0.7″; Jamaica Limpets (*Acmaea jamaicensis*), 0.6″. Florida and Caribbean area.

Diana's Ear Shells (*Strombus aurisdianae*), 3.2″. Australia.

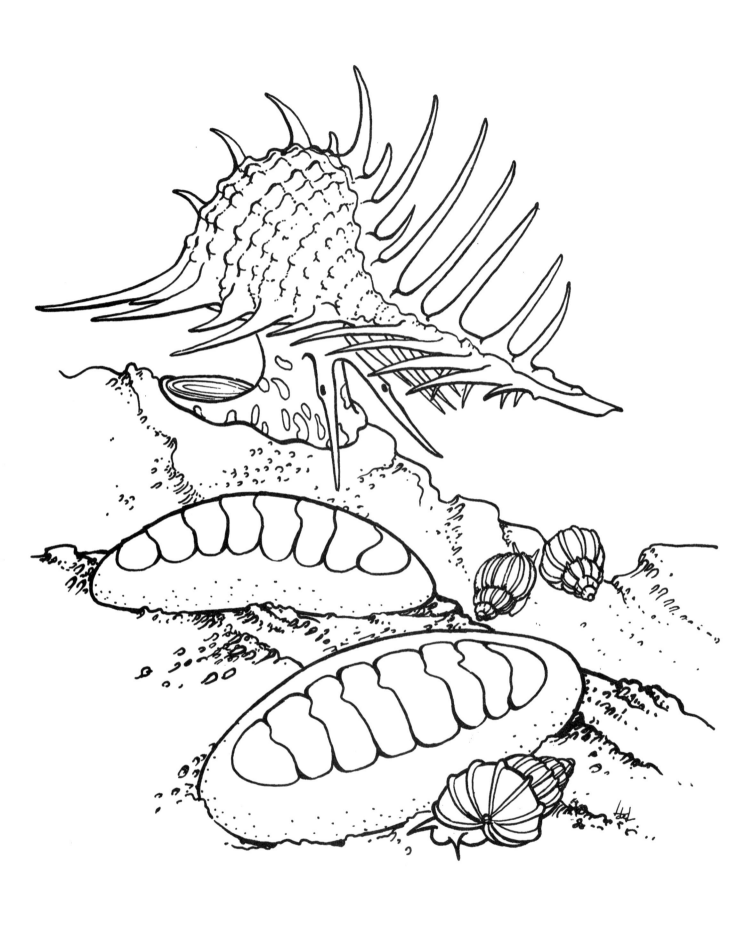

TOP: **Spiny Murex** (*Murex acanthostephes*), 4″. BOTTOM: (large shells) **Jeweled Chitons** (*Acanthozostera gemmata*), up to 5.5″; (small shells) **Pallas Wentletraps** (*Epitonium pallasi*), 1″. Australia.

Great Harp Shells (*Harpa major*), 4″. Indo-Pacific area.

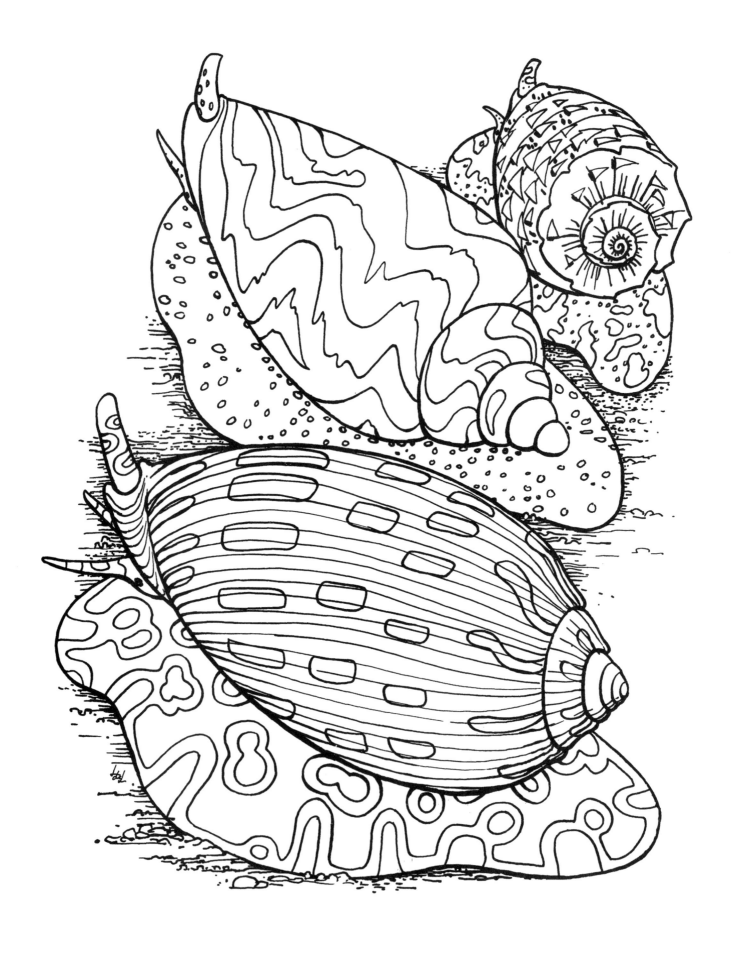

BOTTOM TO TOP: Channeled Volute (*Amoria canaliculata*), 2.4"; Lightning Volute (*Ericusa fulgetrum*), 5.8"; Beautiful Volute (*Cymbiolacca pulchra*), 3.5". Australia.

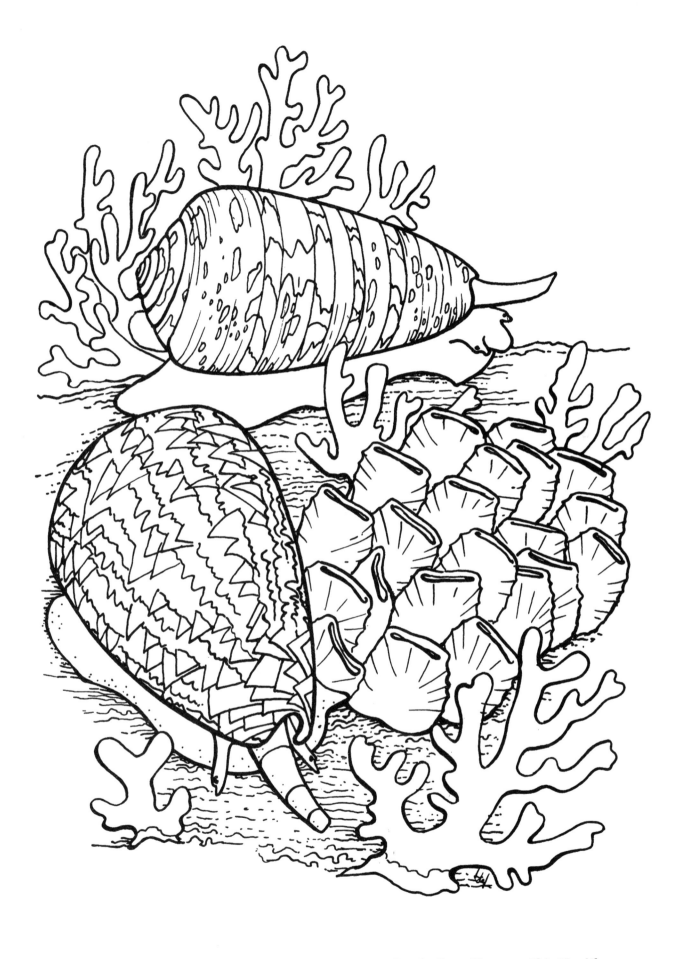

TOP: Anemone Cone (*Conus anemone*), 3.2″. BOTTOM: Textile Cone (*Conus textile*), 4″, with egg capsules. Australia.

123

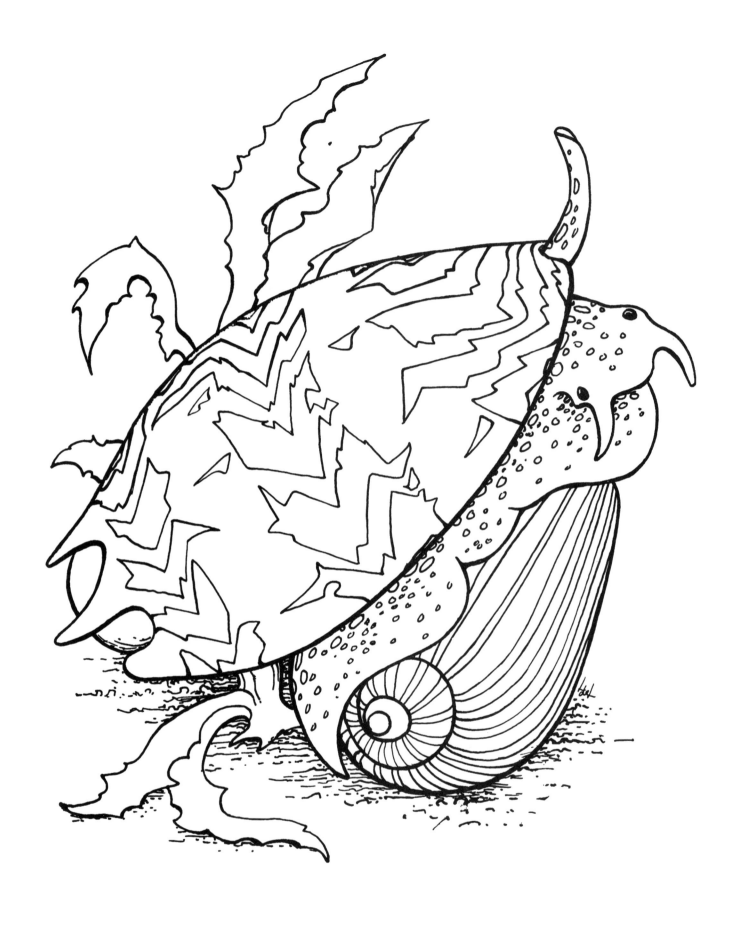

A young Bailer Shell (*Melo amphora*), adult 20″, about to eat a Zebra Volute (*Amoria zebra*), 2″. Australia.

LEFT: Rusty Limpet (*Patella ferruginea*), 2.5″. RIGHT: Waved Helmet (*Semicassis undulata*), 3.5″. Mediterranean.

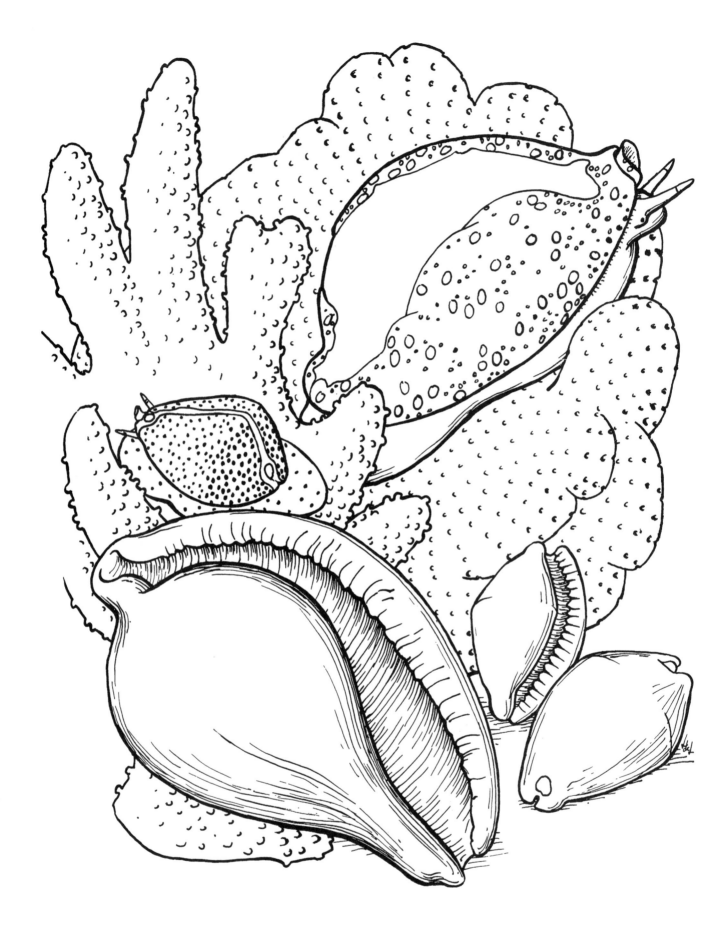

TWO LARGE SHELLS: Egg Cowries (*Ovula ovum*), 3″, with mantle partially extended (top) and an empty shell. THREE SMALL SHELLS: Warted Egg Shells (*Calpurnus verrucosus*), 1″, with mantle extended (left) and empty shells. Mediterranean.

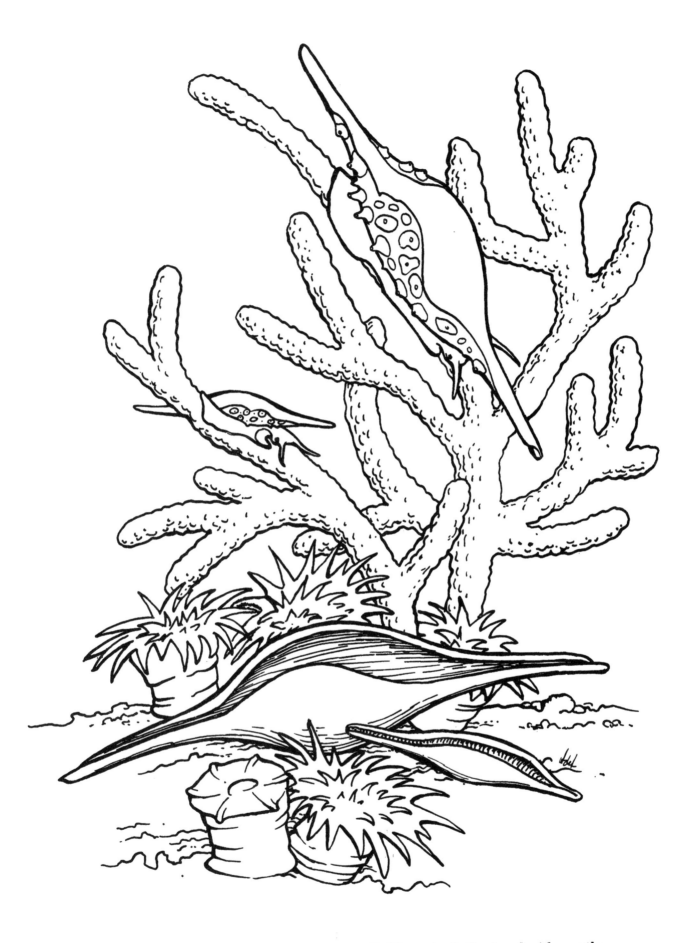

TWO LARGE SHELLS: Shuttlecocks (*Volva volva*), 3″–5″, empty (bottom) and with mantle partially extended (top). TWO SMALL SHELLS: Roseate Egg Shells (*Phenacovolva brevirostris*), 1″, empty (bottom) and with mantle partially extended (above). Australia.

FOUR SMALL SHELLS: Communal Nerite shells (*Neritina communis*), 1″. MIDDLE: Sundial Shell (*Architectonica maxima*), 2.5″. TOP: Golden Cowry (*Cypraea aurantium*), 4″. Indo-Pacific area.

TOP: Gray's Volute (*Amoria grayi*), 4″. BOTTOM: Spotted Volute (*Amoria maculata*), 3.2″. Australia.

Gartered Cone (*Conus genuanus*), 2". West Africa.

Donkey's Ear Abalone (*Haliotis asinina*), 3". Australia.

Measled Cowries (*Cypraea zebra*), 3″, empty shells and live cowry with mantle extended over shell. Florida and Caribbean area.

Giant Clams (*Tridacna gigas*), 2′–4′, empty shell and two live clams showing mantle (top). Indo-Pacific area.

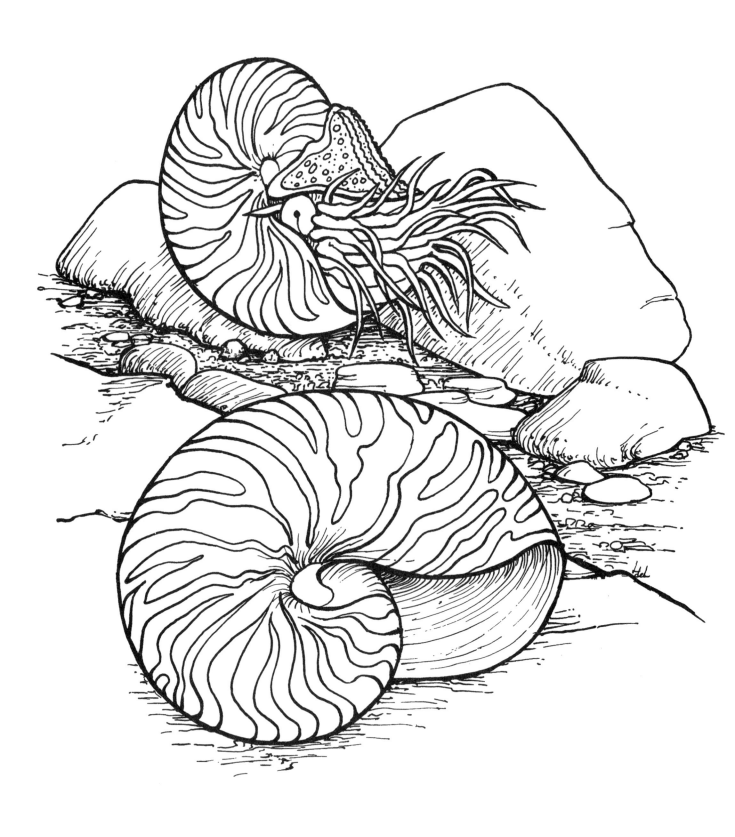

Chambered Nautilus (*Nautilus pompilius*), 4″–8″. Indo-Pacific area.

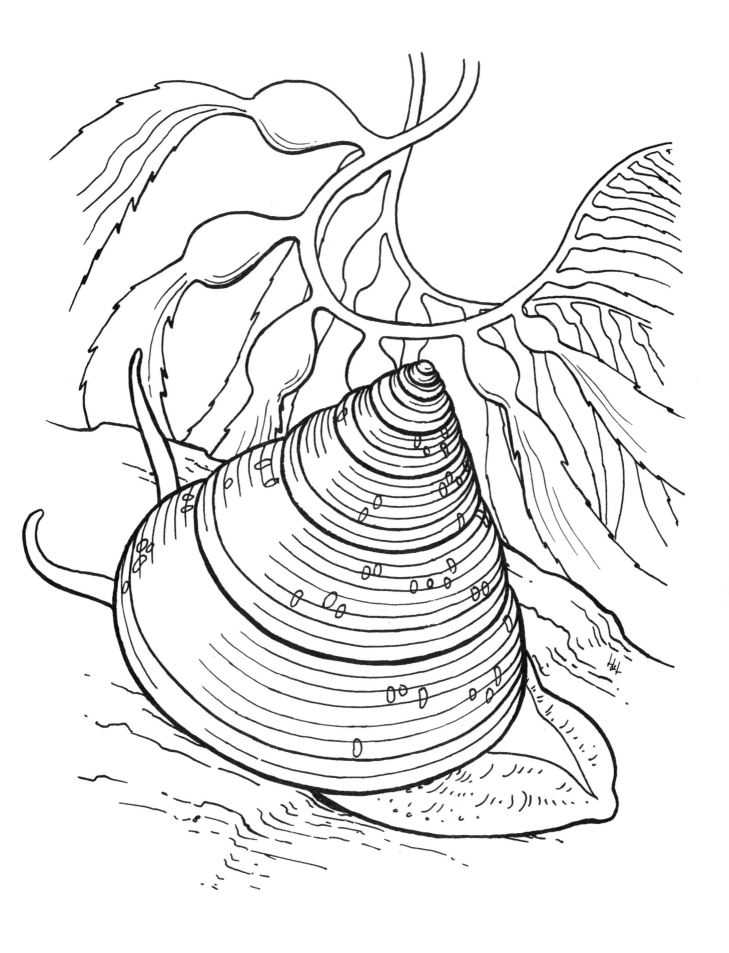

Ringed-Top Shell (*Calliostoma annulatum*), 1.2″. California.

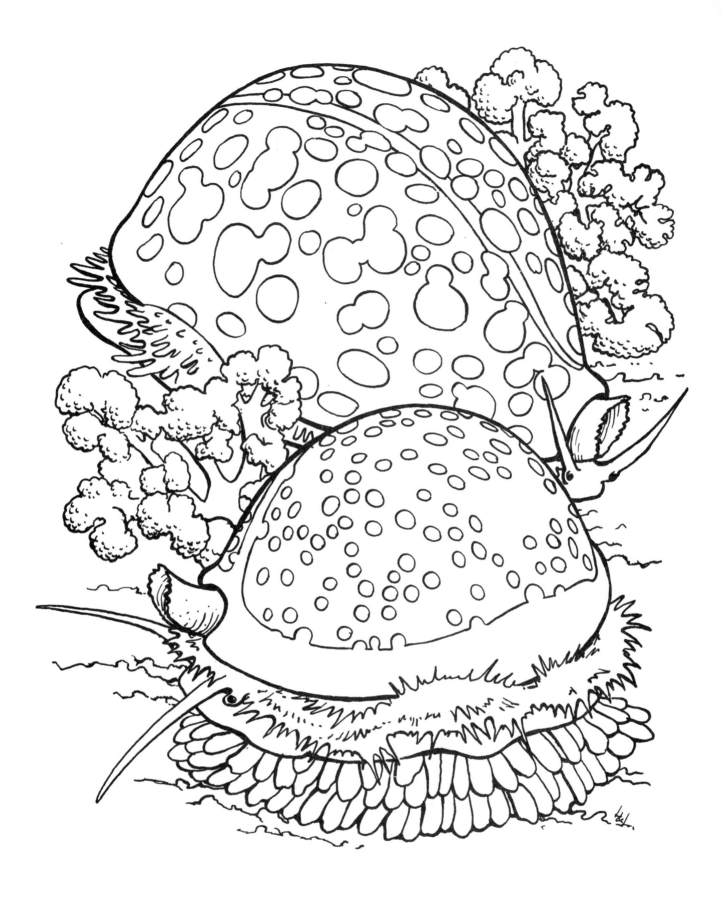

TOP: **Tiger Cowry** (*Cypraea tigris*), 3″. BOTTOM: **Millet Cowry** (*Cypraea miliaris*), 1.2″, ventilating egg capsules. Indo-Pacific area.

BOTTOM TO TOP: Emperor's Slit Shell (*Pleurotomaria hirasei*), 3″–5″; Noble Scallop (*Pecten nobilis*), 3″–5″; Triseriate Auger (*Terebra triseriata*), 3″–5″; Noble Scallop; Lightning Cones (*Conus fulmen*), 2.3″. Japan.

TOP: Australian Scallop (*Mimachlamys subgloriosa*), 3″. BOTTOM: Red Cockles (*Nemocardium bechei*), 2.5″. Australia.

BOTTOM: Bull-Mouth Helmet (*Cypraecassis rufa*), 4″–6″. TOP: Bat Volutes (*Voluta vespertilio*), 2″–4″. Indo-Pacific area.

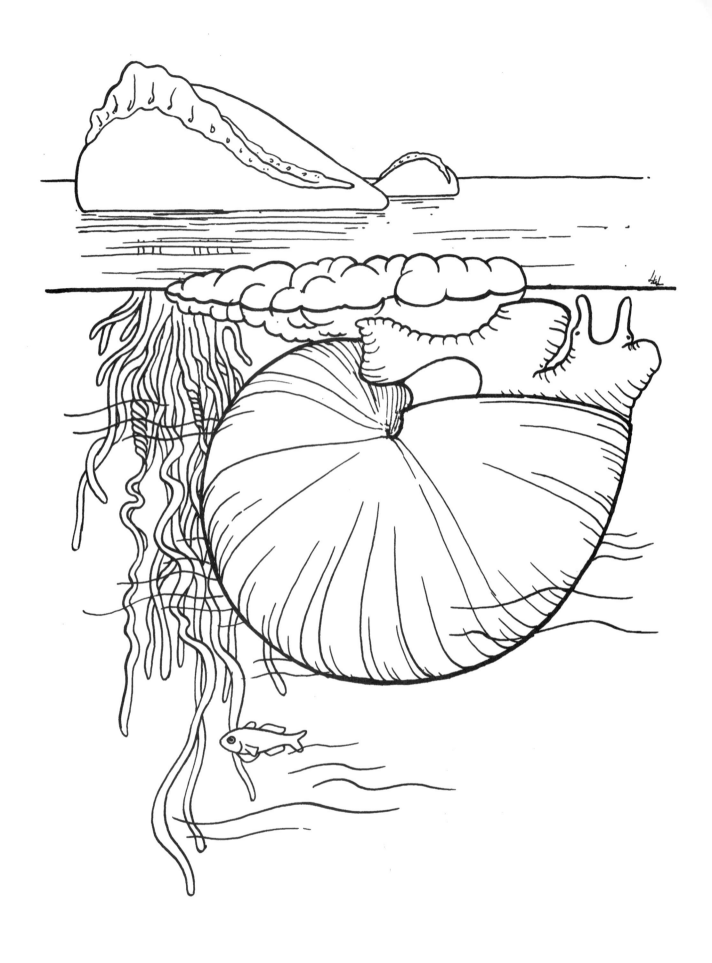

Violet Sea Snail (*Janthina janthina*), 1″, floating on surface with bubbles near a Portuguese Man-of-War. Florida and Caribbean area.

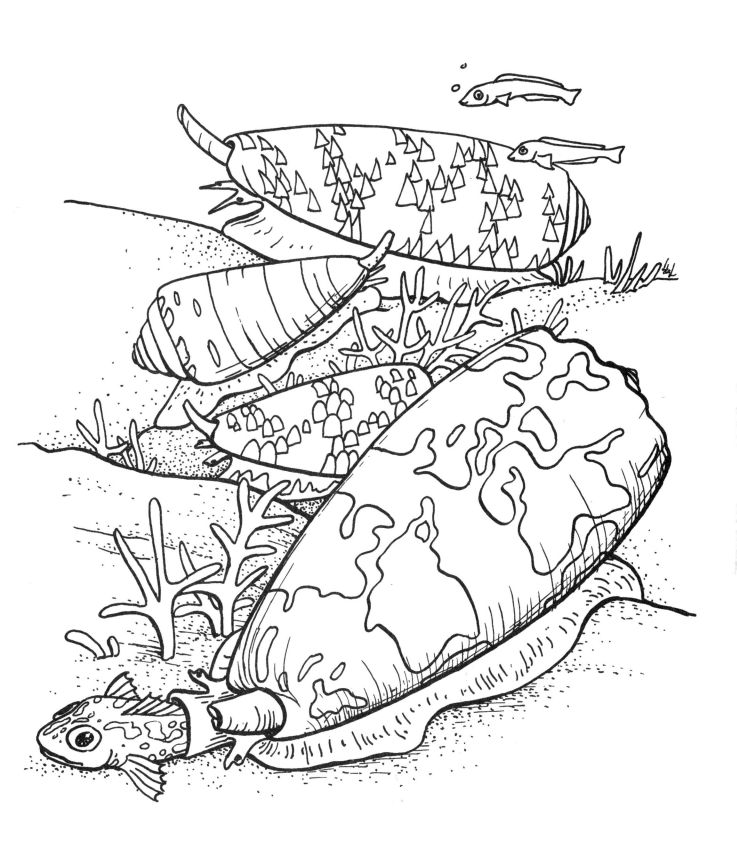

BOTTOM TO TOP: Striate Cone (*Conus striatus*), 2.5″, eating a Blenny fish; Oma Cone (*Conus omaria*), 1.8″; Orange-Banded Cone (*Conus aurisiacus*), 1.8″; Courtly Cone (*Conus aulicus*), 5″. Indo-Pacific area.

De Burgh's Latiaxis (*Latiaxis deburghiae*), 1". Japan.